Dar
Pastor

A PRACTICAL MANUAL FOR
EQUIPPING DANCERS TO
RELEASE THE KINGDOM OF HEAVEN

SAARA TAINA

ISBN-10: 1514823357
ISBN-13: 978-1514823354

Acknowledgements

Thank You, God, for Your constant counsel and comfort on this adventure of life. Thank You for placing so many amazing people along my path to journey with.

Thank you, Mom and Dad, for always being there for me and for helping me look to Jesus in every circumstance. Thank you Eeva and Tony – my sister and brother-in-law – and Eero and Claudia – my brother and sister-in-law – for your constant encouragement.

Thank you, Pastor Bill and Beni Johnson, Pastor Kris and Kathy Vallotton, and all the wonderful leaders at Bethel. It has been such a joy to serve under your covering. Many thanks to the Bethel Healing Rooms leaders, Chris Gore and Chuck Parry, for creating such a fun and empowering environment to explore all that God has for us. Thank you Bethel Activation Ministry (B.A.M.) leaders, Joaquin and Renee Evans, for building a practical covering and safe community for all of us crazy revivalists. Thank you, Ann Mack, Director of Dance at Bethel Church, for all the work you have pioneered and the foundation you have built. Thanks for inviting me to partner with you. Thank you, Theresa Dedmon, Director of Creative Arts at Bethel Church, for releasing me to run with the vision to equip the nations to worship Jesus with all they are. Thank you, Kristene DiMarco and Joanna Finchum, worship pastors in Bethel School of Supernatural Ministry (BSSM), for giving me and my dance teams freedom to explore what God can do in corporate worship settings through dance. And a special thank you to all the BSSM and Bethel Healing Rooms dancers for joining me in this grand adventure to release the Kingdom of God through dance!

Thank you, Annette Biggers, for the amazing photos and, Martina Rieben, for the cover design and formatting. Thank you, Melissa Amato, for your beautiful work with editing, and Liesl Gray for your help. So thankful for all of you!

Photo credits:
Cover and Chapters 5, 9 – Annette Biggers
Chapters 1, 2, 4, 6 – Jaakko Taina
Chapter 3 – Jan Fernández Nash
Chapter 7 – Stephen Santos
Chapter 8 – Carmody Homan

Photography by Annette Biggers www.triplecord.com
Graphic Design by Martina Rieben www.martinasarah.com

Endorsements

Both my husband and I have enjoyed having Saara on our dance team at Bethel. We agree that when she dances in worship, it brings joy to the room. You can tell that her devotion to the Lord is pure and holy. There is a beautiful fragrance that she gives. This book, *Dance Pastor,* will help many who have found themselves in a place of pastoring others in dance before the Lord.

Beni Johnson
Senior Leader (with her husband Bill Johnson)
Bethel Church, Redding, CA
http://www.benij.org
Author, *The Happy Intercessor*

Saara and the dancers are an integral part of the freedom in the Bethel Healing Rooms. What they carry and release into the Healing Rooms as they worship the Lord in dance is beyond what I anticipated. Saara does not write this book out of just knowledge, but out of many years of experience. I would encourage anyone that is interested in implementing a dance ministry to read this book which will not only help equip, but will also help you to pastor this amazing ministry.

Chris Gore
Director of Healing Ministries
Bethel Church, Redding, CA
www.kingdomreleasers.org
Author, *Walking in Supernatural Healing Power*

Dancing can be a scary subject for pastors to release in their church if they don't have the adequate tools for building a dance community based on honor, purity, and experience. Saara's manual will give any church the tools needed to see a dance ministry begin, as well as help with existing dance ministries. I would not only highly recommend this manual, but I furthermore believe it will be a bridge to awaken the church to see how powerful dance can be in the congregation, healing rooms setting, and schools of ministry. After a few pages, you will be hooked!

Theresa Dedmon
Director of Creative Arts
Bethel Church, Redding, CA
http://createsupernaturally.com
Author, *Born to Create*

Saara has this incredible joy that is demonstrated in her dancing and it is contagious. Working alongside of her has provided a profound education in the movement of the Holy Spirit through dance, and how this physical expression creates breakthrough — greater breakthrough than if dance was not present in worship. I've always associated dance with only "perfectly free" people, but Saara approaches it as a journey into freedom. I know you will be encouraged by her process and find yourself lost in love with Jesus.

Kristene DiMarco

2nd Year Worship Pastor

Bethel School of Supernatural Ministry, Redding, CA

www.jesusculturemusic.com

Table of Contents

Preface

I remember so vividly the puzzled look on the government official's face when he was reading my R-1 visa application papers at the U.S. Consulate in Helsinki, Finland. He lifted his eyes from the paperwork and asked, with a smirk on his face, *"You are a Dance Pastor? What does that mean?"* I honestly don't remember what I answered, but he must have picked up the hesitation in my voice because he quickly continued, *"Don't worry, your paperwork is already approved. I'm just curious to know what a dance pastor does."* I must have laughed nervously and given him some sort of a reply, but I knew I was on a journey to discover for myself what it looks like to pastor dancers. Quite likely I was the first person in history to have been granted a religious worker visa on the basis of being an ordained "Dance Pastor."

In writing this manual, my aim is to shed some light on this topic based on my experiences. Whether you are in a consulate, a dance studio, the market place, or a church, my hope is that you'll be equipped with some answers if you happen to be asked the question, *"What is a dance pastor?"* Even more importantly, I hope you will receive some practical tools for doing your job well!

1

Becoming a Dance Pastor

Stepping into your calling always happens in partnership with God; He initiates and we respond. He reaches out and we grab hold of His hand. As we respond to His call and offer Him our all, His breath makes us come fully alive. When we trust Him with our "lunch basket" (like the little fellow did in Matthew 14), He releases His unending grace. The moment we start sharing with others, everything we have multiplies until we have more than enough. In my own journey, I have discovered it all comes down to trust. Trusting God is like letting Him lead the dance. Trust is more than just a feeling — it's accepting the invitation to partner with Him, with your heart wide open. His partnership is delightful and makes you look like an expert.

Those of you who have read my previous book *Encountering God Through Dance* are familiar with my personal journey of how dance came into my life. I won't repeat it all, but I'd like to give you a quick recap to help you understand my background. I started out as a gymnast and didn't really have any grid for dance or dance ministry. I have received many prophetic words throughout my life that God would use me to release His presence all over the world through dance, yet it has been a long journey to discover what this means. Let's pick up where I left off in my first book.

I studied dance for three years in Sydney, Australia, and earned an Advanced Diploma of Creative Arts in Christian Ministry, majoring in contemporary dance. In a sense, I had made myself ready and prepared my own "lunch basket" as well as I knew how. But I needed the hand of God to bless what I carried in order for it to really become a blessing for others as well. I knew none of my dreams would come true without His anointing and touch. In my first book, I shared that after studying dance in Sydney, I came to Bethel Church in Redding, California. I have been pastoring the dance teams in Bethel's Healing Rooms for several years now. I have also been leading and overseeing the dance ministry teams in Bethel School of Supernatural Ministry (BSSM) the past couple of years. In my previous book, I didn't share how all of this happened. The formerly hidden part of my story follows.

While I was living in Australia, I went on a ministry trip to Israel during one of my school holidays. A few years before this trip, I had attended the School of Worship in Jerusalem and lived there for a year, so I had several friends there. On this ministry trip, I went to the first One Thing Young Adult Conference in Jerusalem, which was later renamed the Elav Conference. It was very special to do some dance ministry there, but it felt like I ended up receiving much more than I actually gave. During this trip, God started speaking with me about going to Bethel. I had heard about Bethel through good friends of mine from Norway who had visited Redding, California. My friends had sent me some recordings of Pastor Bill Johnson, and his teaching was feeding my spirit in such a refreshing way.

On this particular trip to Israel, I met a ministry team from Bethel. Joaquin Evans was one of the speakers at this conference, and I actually was healed from a chronic neck condition in a meeting where he was ministering. Little did I know that in a few years he would be one of my leaders, first in the Bethel Healing Rooms, then later in Bethel Activation Ministries (B.A.M.), but I did start to get the feeling that I hadn't run into this Bethel team by accident.

After the conference, I stayed in Israel a little longer. July 22, 2007 ended up being a very memorable day. I'm usually not very good at remembering dates, but this one I wrote down so I wouldn't forget it. I was spending time with God when, all of a sudden, a particular verse "jumped" at me from the pages of my Bible! It was totally out of its original context, but I knew the Holy Spirit was playfully highlighting this verse for me. It said, *"So one of the priests ... came to live in Bethel and taught them how to worship the Lord"* (2 Kings 17:28). I had to admit this was kind of a strange word, but in my heart of hearts I believed God had spoken it to me. I believed God would open the door for me to come to Bethel in His timing, and I would get to teach and demonstrate how to worship God through dance. More specifically, I would have the opportunity to teach how to worship Him with everything we are — spirit, soul, and body — and release an impartation for worship dance.

What was I to do with a word like that? You can't exactly go to a place and introduce yourself as the person God is sending to them. I decided to keep this word in my heart. I figured if God was really sending me, He would clearly lead me and open the doors for me.

In December 2008 I graduated from the School of Creative Arts in Sydney, Australia. On my way home to Finland I had a layover in California. At this time, my brother, Eero, was doing his first year at BSSM, so I thought this was a great opportunity for me to visit Bethel and see my brother. I knew there was no such thing on earth as a perfect church, but I also knew our spirit could sense if we are welcomed in a place or not. When I came to my very first service at Bethel, I had no doubt I had come home. Pastor Bill Johnson was preaching on the scripture about the sheep hearing the voice of their shepherd. It obviously refers to us hearing God's voice, but we can also discern the voice of our earthly pastors and know where we belong. I knew I had just heard the voice of my pastor.

After this visit, I knew I needed to be at Bethel. I don't think Bethel is superior to other churches, or by any means the only place where God is moving. I have seen Him move in many locations around the world, but it was evident God was leading me to Bethel. There is no better place for us to be than where He is planting us. I could taste and see these people were truly after God's heart. I was just hungry for the presence of God and didn't want anything else but to be saturated by His presence. While growing up, I had received so many prophetic words about releasing God's presence and His miracle working power through dance all around the world. I had done my part in preparing myself for His calling on my life, but I knew without His touch and a strong community of believers, none of my dreams would ever come true.

I did have a bit of a practical dilemma, though. I needed a visa to come to the States, and it seemed like the only option for me was to come as a student to BSSM and apply for a student visa. By this time, I had already been to several ministry schools and been in full-time ministry for many years, including doing dance ministry on five different continents. I knew many people would think I had lost my mind if I went to another ministry school, but there was no turning back. I knew I needed to go. Thankfully my parents were very supportive and understanding, like they have been throughout my whole life.

BSSM ended up being a huge blessing, so I was glad I had been required to do the school in order to get a visa. I didn't tell anyone at school about the word I had received a few years earlier. I just positioned my heart to receive everything God had for me, keeping my eyes on Him. A place where I really came alive was the Bethel Healing Rooms. I was able to join the dance ministry team the very first week I came to Redding. This actually demonstrated God's favor because usually students are not allowed to join the ministry teams until after the first semester. Our little dance team was just worshiping and getting lost in God's presence for several hours every Saturday. I loved every part of it and never missed a Saturday. After a couple of months, I was asked to start co-leading the Bethel Healing Rooms dance team.

Besides the Healing Rooms dance team, which was very small at the time, there weren't really other opportunities to be involved in dance ministry. There were no worship dance teams in BSSM. The church had a small dance team that ministered occasionally, but it was a closed team without a way to apply or audition to be part of it. There weren't any open dance classes at church either, but I was actually very thankful for this season of hiddenness. I could just focus on loving God and letting Him love me back. During both the school's corporate worship times and church worship times, I would find a little spot somewhere in the very back of the sanctuary where I could express my heart to Jesus. All the meetings were so crowded that there wasn't really much room to move, but somehow I always managed to find my own little spot where I could dance. It reminded me of the very first time I started dancing in worship about ten years earlier. My first year at BSSM held many sweet and memorable moments, but also funny ones — bumping into people or quite literally falling into the arms of an unassuming student who was trying to pass by in the crowded room.

Besides some comical moments due to the small space, I had some radical, life-changing encounters with Jesus. I remember tangibly feeling His presence several times and letting Him lead the dance. God was reminding me that the ultimate pilgrimage and the uttermost privilege in life is to journey into the depths of the heart of my Father — to know the feelings of His heart and to dance to the rhythm of His heartbeat. God wooed me back into that place of first love. The biggest revelation I received during my first year of BSSM was the most basic one: There is no life outside of His love, and when I hear His love song, I can't help but respond. That's how the dance begins and that's how it has always begun.

Nearly five years later, I found out my worship times also had an impact on other students. Last year I was invited to do a dance ministry trip to Colorado for an event that was run by a couple from my first year class. The husband shared how they had been facing some very challenging circumstances and, throughout our whole first year, he had stood in the back of the sanctuary, cried, and watched me worship. He said seeing me worship had really taught him what worship is about, and this revelation was one of the keys that had carried him through that difficult season. Until he shared this with me years later, I had no idea how my worship had impacted him. In some of our "hidden" seasons, we may not be as hidden as we think we are.

A few months into my first year of BSSM, a lady walked up to me after a time of worship. She introduced herself as one of the home group leaders at Bethel. She said she had been sensing the anointing through my dance, and was wondering if I could come and dance at one of her home group meetings. I told her I would be happy to come, but within the next couple of days she sent me a few e-mails that made me feel slightly nervous. She told me I would need to come alone, be there at a certain time, dance to a piece of instrumental music for 3-4 minutes, and then leave right after. I don't know how you would feel, but I was sort of freaked out by these instructions. I actually looked her up on Google to make sure she was a legitimate home group leader. After my research, I found out she was "official," and because I had already promised to come, I figured I should just do it. However, I asked a friend of mine to wait in the car in a nearby area just in case I needed to be rescued.

When I arrived at the house where the home group was held, this lady came to meet me outside. She told me the reason why she had given me such specific instructions was that she had also invited Beni Johnson (Bill and Beni Johnson are the Senior Leaders of Bethel Church). This home group was focused on dream interpretation and the prophetic, and she had invited Beni to come and interpret my dance. She also told me she wanted to introduce me to the leaders at Bethel so they could see what I carry. She didn't want to tell me this beforehand so I wouldn't get nervous, but the not-getting-nervous part didn't quite work out the way she had thought it would. I may have actually been less nervous if I had known in advance what was going on. Regardless of the unusual set up, this ended up being a very significant meeting.

There were only a handful of people in the living room, and Pastor Beni sat in the middle of the room on a big chair. The only other time I had actually talked with her was when I first arrived at Bethel. I had run into her in the bathroom of the prayer chapel, completely oblivious of who she was. I remember her initiating a casual conversation, asking me what my name was and where I was from, and in return I had asked what her name was. It didn't dawn on me until afterward that she was "the" Beni — the Senior Leader at the church I had just come to! She must have been amused by my ignorance. I still blush when thinking about it. So much for first impressions. Obviously I wasn't at Bethel to impress her, or anyone else for that matter.

They had made some space for me to dance on one side of the room. I hadn't really thought through what I was going to do, but I gave them my iPod to play a track from one of my instrumental CDs. I can't even remember which song it was, and it's sort of irrelevant, but I knew in my spirit the theme for my dance was surrender. I remember closing my eyes and thinking, *"God, either You will show up, or this is going to be ridiculous."* He did show up. The moment I started dancing, I completely forgot the awkwardness of the whole situation. I quite literally threw myself into God's arms and danced with Him.

Afterward, Beni was asked to interpret my dance. The first thing she said was that the whole dance was about surrender! This was quite mind-blowing for me to hear since there were no lyrics or other indication that would have allowed her to know this was exactly what I was communicating. She also pointed out several specific parts throughout the dance, and explained what had happened there. This was the first time anyone had ever interpreted my dance. I was so impacted by the accuracy because my spirit resonated with everything she said.

Fairly soon after this event, I was invited to join the worship dance team at Bethel. I don't know if Beni put in a good word for me, or if something just shifted in the spirit realm, making the doors fling wide open. In any case, this was really the turning point for me. All of a sudden I stepped out of a place of hiddenness into quite an intense season of ministry opportunities everywhere. In navigating through these different seasons, God has been teaching me what a true partnership with Him looks like. He really is faithful to His promises and wants us to enjoy Him in every season of our lives. I never need to promote myself, but as in every partnership, I'm never just passively waiting and doing nothing. Even though in this dance of life my part is seemingly tiny compared with God's part, it's very needed. God can't lead the dance unless I'm responding by moving with Him. My role is to trust Him and keep on taking steps. Much like learning to dance, life is not so much about getting the steps right — it's about lifting up your eyes and letting your heart come out. And when you are close to Him, He is more than able to lead you.

When God is calling you to something, He will make a way as you partner with Him, even in times when there seems to be no way. He specializes in making roads in unknown, unfamiliar places. Part of the miracle for me was getting a new visa after graduating from BSSM so I could stay in the U.S. During my third year of BSSM, I pioneered the dance ministry teams within our school of ministry. I was overseeing the worship dance teams in the 2nd year class and developing a weekly dance outreach team. Theresa Dedmon, who I was interning for, invited me to stay and continue as a volunteer to build the dance community within BSSM. Being from overseas without having employment can be a bit of a challenge, especially when it comes to visas. Yet God showed Himself faithful again. I traveled back to my home country, Finland, to apply for a new visa. While I was there, someone kindly gave me a gift card to a travel agency so I could book a flight back to California. The process for getting permission to apply for a visa took so long that my gift card was about to expire. In fact, I stayed in Finland for four months, not knowing if I would get a visa or not.

This time of waiting was emotionally very stretching. I had been through many transitions in the previous years and had learned to adapt to different cultures. But this time was different because I had to deal with the culture shock of being back in my home country after living abroad for years. I also had to deal with many curious people who were wondering what I was doing with my life. I was a 33-year-old woman who was moving back into her parents' house, which was enough for some of my friends to question my choices, and for the enemy to attempt to ridicule me. Thankfully I discovered I had many true friends who were extremely supportive and simply delighted I was back. It ended up being an incredible time of connecting with people back home. It was truly another opportunity to learn how to completely surrender to God, gaining more experiential knowledge of His perfect timing.

The day before my gift card for booking flights expired, I still hadn't received an answer for the visa petition Bethel had done for me. My mom had told me she felt like God would give me the answer before my gift card expired. She reminded me that God had given it to me specifically for my trip to California. My level of faith wasn't quite there yet. I didn't want to waste the gift card, so I started contacting friends in different countries, wondering if anyone would like a surprise guest from Finland. The morning came when I needed to book a flight, and I decided to check my e-mail for a visa update one last time before giving up. Those of you who walk in the same level of faith as my mom can probably guess what happened. The e-mail declaring the faithfulness of God had indeed arrived — my petition had been approved! This meant I could now book my visa interview and more importantly, book my flight. It was still a little leap of faith, since I didn't have my actual visa yet. However, the timing was so incredible that now I was fully ready to jump. I packed up all my earthly belongings, said goodbye once again to family and friends back home, and booked my flight to California. Then I rode on a train for 11 hours to go to Helsinki for a visa interview. I know most people would do the visa interview before packing up everything, booking flights, and saying goodbye. I guess my mom's faith had finally started to rub off on me! This time my spirit was convinced God was sending me back to California.

As you probably guessed, I received my visa without problems, even though the immigration officials were seemingly amused by the title "Dance Pastor." I had some great definitions in my paperwork for my position as a dance pastor, but it has been quite a journey learning what this title means in practical terms. The ironic part is I knew that God was calling me to train and equip worship dancers, but I had never thought of my role as being very pastoral. I actually needed to be ordained as a pastor because of the type of visa I had. Since this time, I have discovered the pastoral role is an essential and strategic key in building dance ministries. Most of the time when dance ministries fall off their foundation, I think it is due to a lack of pastoral covering. Dancers need to be pastored and spiritually covered in order for them to fully bloom. Everything in this book has been learned through experience. God helped me discover some keys for building dance ministries, and I'm honored to share them with you.

2

Core Value I
The Presence of God

Building Dance Communities

The Bible talks a lot about building. We all are builders in one way or another. We need to ask ourselves what we are building and how we are building it. Since I was a child, I have been fascinated by this parable Jesus shared:

"Therefore everyone who hears these words of Mine and puts them into practice is like a wise man who built his house on the rock. The rain came down, the streams rose, and the winds blew and beat against that house; yet it did not fall, because it had its foundation on the rock. But everyone who hears these words of Mine and does not put them into practice is like a foolish man who built his house on sand. The rain came down, the streams rose, and the winds blew and beat against that house, and it fell with a great crash" (Matthew 7: 24-27).

This reveals to us the importance of considering the foundation when we build. It's a simple enough principle that even little kids can grasp it, but too often we are in such a rush when building ministries that we forget to check if we are building on the right ground. Some of these "buildings" may look absolutely gorgeous on the outside, yet we often hear of ministries falling down with quite a crash when the first little storm hits them. Seeing this happen to dance ministries has always made me feel sad, and preventing it is one of the reasons why I'm so passionate about learning to build on a good foundation.

In this parable, Jesus wasn't talking directly about building ministries, but the same principle still applies. Jesus was talking about radical obedience — hearing His words and putting them into practice. If you're starting something new, it's always a good idea to begin by listening to His voice. It's an even better idea to not only begin this way, but to be constantly leaning toward His heart and hearing His heart beat. He really is the Master builder and knows what He's doing.

The book of Psalms says, *"Unless the Lord builds the house, the builders labor in vain"* (Psalm 127:1a). Does the Lord build the house or do we? The answer is yes. It's both — the Lord builds the house and so do we. We are called to co-labor with Him. That's the only way to build something that lasts and has eternal value. Many important factors are present when building dance communities in a church or in other settings. My focus is on the ones God has been highlighting to me while pastoring the dance teams in BSSM and in the Bethel Healing Rooms. I will explore various aspects of different types of dance ministries in more detail later on in this book.

One key to building a solid foundation is having, and living according to, core values. I have been applying four core values in all of the dance ministries I have been overseeing. They are like the four legs of a chair — if one is missing, things become shaky very quickly, and if two or more are missing, it's not a fun ride. You can apply all of these principles to any kind of dance ministry: 1) Presence of God, 2) Partnership with One Another, 3) Pursuing Excellence, 4) Pastoral Covering.

Focusing on God's Presence

Each of these core values will be explored in more detail in the following chapters. The rest of this chapter focuses on the Presence of God. We don't want to do anything outside of God's presence. It's His presence and His anointing that break negative yokes, and release healing, freedom, and all kinds of breakthrough. Our creative expressions should come from a place of communing with God — an external overflow of our internal connection and relationship with Him.

Moses said to God, *"If your Presence does not go with us, do not send us up from here. How will anyone know that You are pleased with me and with Your people unless You go with us? What else will distinguish me and Your people from all the other people on the face of the earth?"* (Exodus 33:15-16).

God's presence continues to be the distinguishing mark on us. His presence sets us apart from other dance groups. If we don't have His presence, we end up being like soap bubbles – beautiful to watch, but lasting only for a moment before popping without any eternal impact.

God is love. The Scriptures are very clear about this. *"Whoever does not love does not know God, because God is love"* (1 John 4:8). God can't be anything but loving, because love is the essence of who He is. In the same way, we can't help but walk in love if we are carriers of His presence. God's presence and His love are inseparable. Jesus Himself said, *"By this everyone will know that you are My disciples, if you love one another"* (John 13:35).

Love is the very first fruit of the Spirit mentioned in Galatians 5:22, and it's the evidence that we are truly walking with God and carrying His presence. Powerful imagery about the importance of love is given in 1 Corinthians 13. Without love, our communication, whether in tongues of men or angels, ends up being just like a *"resounding gong or a clashing cymbal."* Just noise — empty, annoying noise. Dance is also a way to communicate. Without love, our language of movement ends up also being empty and annoying. I have a friend whose little boys used to mix up the two words "anointing" and "annoying." When we don't flow from love, our dance can easily become annoying instead of anointed.

God's presence creates an atmosphere of love. I was recently reading through some feedback forms from the 1st year BSSM students on the Healing Rooms dance team. One of the dancers wrote this comment, referring to her experience on the dance team: *"It was one of my highlights this year. I have had a real struggle with stepping out and dancing with the Holy Spirit, but with the dance team, it was so natural and easy. I have never been in a dance environment like this before, where there's no performance or competition to be the best."*

In order to create this kind of environment, everyone needs to cultivate God's presence in their own lives and take responsibility for their personal relationship with God. However, as leaders and pastors, it's very important to set a standard and represent God's heart well. It's a constant pursuit after His heart. We don't want to ever be in a place of passivity in our relationship with Him. Loving God and loving others is an ongoing journey. It's not about striving. It's about learning to connect with His heart and locking our eyes with Him. He is our source.

God's presence can be manifested in so many ways. I could give you a long list of powerful testimonies of healings and miracles we have seen through dance ministry. I will be sharing some of these stories later on, but I believe the most powerful manifestation of His presence is genuine love. Don't get me wrong, as a dance community we are pressing into seeing more and more of the miraculous power of God. But the way it happens is through love — by leaning into the heart of God and being filled with His love. Love never fails.

When I teach dance classes to my dance team members, the main focus is always helping them learn how to move from a place of intimacy with God — from their heart to heart connection with Him. Below are a few practical examples of ways to help dancers experience and grow in this. These are by no means the only exercises for this, and I hope they inspire you to develop your own ideas for activating dancers in their awareness of God's presence as they minister.

Exercise 1. The Rain

I learned this exercise from Jane Farrelly, who was one of my amazing dance teachers when I studied dance in Sydney, Australia at School of Creative Arts. Several years prior to this, she had battled with cancer. In the midst of the battle, God showed her a vision. He used this vision to heal her. Later, in complete recovery, she translated the vision into a contact dance improvisation format.

The vision had three parts:

1) Jane was released from the grip of cancer as the rain of the Holy Spirit washed over her.

Testimony: It was as if I stood absolutely still whilst a very gentle, and gloriously beautiful, sun shower brought the love and light of God into my whole being.

2) Father God came and stood alongside her and swayed her gently in His arms.

Testimony: This was experienced as letting go and letting God — a true surrender to God as I let Him take away all my pain, heaviness, and heartache.

3) Jesus stood in front of her, reached out His hand, and invited her to dance with Him.

Testimony: With small movements at first, Jesus gradually took me to a place of complete healing. Jesus enabled me to move in step with the Holy Spirit. Now I am set free to dance in renewed strength in prayer, with thanksgiving, and the highest praise and worship.

A slightly moderated version of the exercise follows. You can find the original version in her thesis, entitled "Dance and Healing," at http://handle.uws.edu.au:8081/1959.7/804.

Arrangements:

Participants work in duos.

All duos come together and form two concentric circles, and everyone in the group faces toward the center of the circles.

One partner stands in the outer circle, and their duo partner is positioned directly in front of them to form their part of the inner circle.

Role-plays:

The leader acts as a participant positioned in the outer circle and works with a partner in order to demonstrate what to do for the other dancers. "You" throughout this entire exercise, as well as the rest of the exercises, refers to you as the leader.

The person in the outer circle is called the "giver" and represents God. All givers keep their eyes open throughout the whole exercise.

The person in the inner circle is being ministered to and is called the "receiver." All receivers are free to close their eyes during the First and Second Phase of the exercise.

First Phase – duration approximately three minutes

This First Phase introduces three different contact movement experiences.

Part A – light relaxing touch (contact through a gentle fingertip "sun shower" of raindrops from the head all the way to the toes):

1. The giver positions their hands with palms softly together directly above the head of the receiver. *You can encourage the giver to pray a blessing quietly over the receiver.*

2. The giver opens both hands over the receiver's head and lightly touches the receiver's head with soft fingertips, moving as gently as light rain. A sun shower is a light rain shower that falls while the sun is shining. *Welcome the warm light of both the sun and the Son.* The "raindrops" cover the receiver from the head to the neck, then across the shoulders, and down the arms and hands. *Welcome the rain of the Holy Spirit to come and wash over the receiver.*

3. Next the raindrops cover the entire back and the back of the legs. The feet are the last to receive the raindrops. *Invite the Holy Spirit to fill them up from the top of their head to the bottom of their feet.*

These first three steps can be repeated two or three times.

Part B – firm grounding of the heel bones, spreading down into the feet and toes:

1. The giver shapes one hand around the back of each heel bone of the receiver, squeezing several times with a gentle, firm, downward pressure. *You can pray over their feet, declaring they are firmly planted on God's Word and His truth, and nothing will move or shake them.*

2. The giver smooths the feet of the receiver with several strokes of their hands over the upper surface of the feet, connecting the feet to the floor gently with a firm, downward pressure. *You can bless their feet to walk and dance in the freedom and joy of the Holy Spirit.*

Part C – release through one tension-release pass:

1. The giver reaches up above the head of the receiver with the palms of their hands together. Both the giver and receiver inhale deeply.

2. Both exhale softly and slowly as the giver smoothly and firmly passes both hands from the head, down to the toes, in one continuous movement. *You can make a declaration that the heavy rain of the Holy Spirit is washing over them, making all things new.*

Second Phase – duration approximately two minutes

This Second Phase includes contact and trust in weight bearing.

The givers move inward to stand beside the receivers, and the two circles become one. Everyone begins the Second Phase standing one beside the other in one circle, facing the center of the circle. The participants all continue to work with the same partner.

Coming beside, taking the weight, and swaying:

1. The giver places their arm closest to the receiver around the waist or shoulders depending on body heights. *You can say out loud, "Papa God is standing right here with you."*

2. The receiver leans on the giver and rests their head on the giver's shoulder. The giver may support the receiver's head with their other free hand. *You can say out loud, "The Father is never going to leave you or forsake you. He is fully committed to you."*

3. Both soften and bend their knees a little, as the giver leads a gentle side-by-side, swaying dance movement.

4. The giver returns to the original position standing behind the receiver.

Third Phase – duration approximately three minutes

This phase includes contact by touch, leading, and duo improvisation. The giver steps in front of the receiver, continuing to work with the same partner.

1. The giver takes hold of the hand of the receiver and holds it for a moment. *You can say out loud, "Jesus is coming to dance with you."*

2. The giver leads the receiver out of the circle by gently pulling them by the hand into a free spot in the room. *You can say out loud, "Jesus is leading you into a new place in dance."*

3. The giver lightly touches the shoulders or the sides of the receiver who sways gently from side to side, moving in direct response to the touch.

4. The sways gradually develop into a full, free-swinging motion of the whole body.

5. The giver continues initiating movement by a light touch, using different body parts to initiate the movement. (Hands are usually the easiest, but they can try initiating movement by other body parts: feet, knees, shoulders, elbows, etc.) The giver doesn't need to touch the receiver constantly, but rather give them a couple of different movement initiations by touch, and let the receiver explore different ways of responding. At this point, the receiver is free to start moving around the room. It's up to them how much or how little they want to move as a response to the giver's touch. It's recommended at this point that everyone keeps their eyes open so they don't bump into other dancers in the room.

6. The movement initiation by touch develops into duo improvisation, which can be in any style of free dance, unique for each participant. Even though the giver participates in the dance, the receiver is their main focus throughout the whole exercise.

Debrief:

Allow the giver and the receiver to have a few moments to discuss their experiences.

Transition:

The receiver and the giver then exchange roles, and the whole process is repeated, including the debrief.

My comments on this exercise:

This exercise is an amazing tool for helping people understand the concept of dancing with God, not just for Him. I have used this exercise in several different cultural settings and have seen many people find a new freedom in dance. They start to experience the presence of God, and He encounters them exactly where they are at. His love sets us free to express ourselves, and the fun part is that each of our expressions are so uniquely different. We don't need to try to look like anyone else.

When I dance in worship, I often feel like there are moments when God literally initiates my movement by His touch, and I just respond as I move with Him. There also are moments when I feel like I do the initiation, but He is still right there with me. He dwells in the praises of His people (Psalm 22:3).

This exercise is also a good introduction to help people allow others into their dance space. If you have never danced with others, you may initially find it challenging. The more you do it, the easier it gets, and you will soon discover the joy of partnering with others. *To make everyone feel safe in this exercise, I usually have ladies partner with ladies, and guys partner with guys, unless there are married couples in the group.*

The way this exercise was created releases a powerful testimony of God's healing presence. I have seen many people receive both physical and inner healing through this exercise.

Exercise 2. Heart to Heart

Arrangements:

Have all the dancers lay on their backs on the floor, evenly spread out all around the room. Turn on some soft, instrumental music. You can dim the lights and ask the dancers to close their eyes. *Invite the Holy Spirit to move and have His way in the class.*

First Phase – duration approximately five minutes

Part A – duration approximately two minutes

Ask the dancers to take a couple of deep breaths, relaxing every muscle. Check that they aren't crossing their legs or arms. Their arms should be relaxed on each side of their body, fairly close to their torsos. Their legs should be slightly apart and relaxed on the floor. Encourage them to feel the floor carrying their full weight. *You can ask them to imagine they are lying on Papa God's hand. He is strong enough to carry them, so they don't need to support their own body weight, but rather fully relax.* You (as the leader) can also walk around the room and lay your hands gently on their forehead or their feet.

Part B – *duration approximately three minutes*

Ask the dancers to listen to their bodies and check how their body is feeling. If they feel muscle tension in any part of their body, they can consciously focus on relaxing that muscle. If they have tension in their neck, they can slowly turn their head from side to side. If tension exists in their feet or hands, they can gently move their toes and fingers. If there is tension in their arms, shoulders, or upper back, they can cross their arms across their body (like giving themselves a hug) and take a few deep breaths. If there's tension in their legs or lower back, they can bend their knees by lifting them up together and, with their feet slightly apart on the floor, rock their legs slowly and gently from side to side. *Invite the Holy Spirit to fill every part of their bodies.*

Second Phase – duration approximately five minutes

While the dancers are lying on the floor, ask them to listen to their heart and ask their heart how it is doing. What is their heart feeling? They may be feeling several different emotions, but ask them to narrow it down to one emotion. What is the number one, strongest feeling on their heart, right at this moment? Once they have recognized and acknowledged what they are feeling, have them start slowly moving their bodies and expressing this emotion to God through movement. This is their personal non-verbal prayer to God. It's a time when they can pour out their heart to God in a real and authentic way. Give them the freedom to move as little or as much as they need to or want to.

Third Phase – duration approximately five minutes

Ask the dancers to pause for a moment. They can sit or lie down on the floor, or just stand still. Ask them to be still for a little while and start listening to what's on God's heart. Have them ask God to show them one specific thing that's on His heart for them personally. Then have the dancers express this word with movement. They can start dancing anywhere in the room. Once again, give them freedom to move as little or as much as they want to. If they don't hear anything right away, they can start dancing while listening.

Debrief:

Give the dancers an opportunity to briefly share what they felt God telling them. They can do this in pairs, and if you have time, you can ask if anyone would like to share about their experience with the whole group.

My comments on this exercise:

This exercise is designed to help the dancers connect with God in spirit and in truth, allowing Him to fill every part of their being. One of the goals is to help the participants realize God is interested in them as a whole person. This exercise helps them acknowledge and express to Him how they are doing. I believe worshiping God in truth means we recognize ourselves for who we are, and God for who He is. When we are honest and real with God, we can invite Him to meet us right where we are at. God of course knows everything about us, but we welcome Him on a friendship level into our lives when we choose to be real with Him.

Exercise 3. Love Languages

We all have different ways of experiencing God's presence. Hebrews 5:14b says, *"Those who by reason of use have their senses exercised to discern"* (King James Version). This verse indicates we can exercise our spiritual senses by using them and we can grow in our discernment. Gary Chapman has written a book called *The 5 Love Languages* in which he talks about five different ways we can express love to one another. We all need all of them, but we usually have a tendency to feel like one or two of these languages are our primary ways of receiving love. The whole book is great, and I recommend reading it. For this exercise, you simply need to know the five love languages: physical touch, receiving gifts, quality time, words of affirmation, and acts of service. I created this exercise to help dancers exercise their spiritual senses and discover different ways of how God can speak and minister to them.

Arrangements:

Have all the dancers lie on the floor, evenly spread out around the room. Have five different tracks of instrumental music selected.

First Phase – approximately three minutes

1. Start playing the first track of the instrumental music you have chosen, preferably something playful and happy. Keep the volume low so you can talk while the music is playing. Tell the dancers to imagine they are lying on a beach. There's warm sand underneath them. It's not burning hot, but nice and relaxing. They can start slowly moving around and playing with the sand. It can be helpful to tell the participants to imagine they are five years old so they have more childlike freedom in their expression. They can draw in the sand with their feet, hands, or elbows. They can roll in the sand. Or they can dance however they like dancing on the beach.

2. Ask the dancers to see Jesus coming toward them. Jesus is taking a hold of their hand and starting to dance with them. Ask them to feel how Jesus is initiating some movements, by gently pushing/touching different parts of their body. For example, He might be playfully spinning them around, lifting their arms from underneath their elbows, or lifting their foot with His toes under their heel. *You can refer to the third section of the rain exercise where Jesus was dancing with them.*

Second Phase – approximately three minutes

1. Start playing the second track of the instrumental music you have chosen. Preferably something with a slower tempo. Tell the dancers Jesus is taking hold of their hand and leading them toward the ocean. They jump into the sea with Him. He is pulling them into the deep waters, and because they can do anything with Jesus, they can breathe under water. Jesus invites them to dance with Him under water. Ask them to feel the resistance of water in their movements. They can't make any quick movements, but every movement is very slow and carries strength and energy in it. They can feel the resistance of the water throughout this whole time. The water is deep, but it's not scary because Jesus is right there with them. Then help them realize the ocean is the heart of their Heavenly Father and they are dancing inside of His heart.

2. Tell the dancers Jesus is taking hold of their hand again and pulling them to the very bottom of the ocean. They can imagine they are diving into the depths of the Father's heart. The Father has a gift for them at the very bottom. They can dive all the way down and see what kind of a gift Papa has hidden there for them. It can be an abstract thing, like joy or peace. Or it can be a concrete thing, like a key or a necklace. It can be anything they see the Father giving them right at this moment; no answer is wrong. They can also ask Jesus what this gift is specifically for.

Third Phase – approximately three minutes

1. Start playing the third track of the instrumental music you have chosen. Preferably something melodic with a faster tempo. Tell the dancers Jesus is taking hold of their hand again. He is pulling them up from the ocean. He is lifting them up in the air, and because they can do anything with Jesus, they can fly with Him. They can start dancing with Jesus in the sky. There is no more resistance for the movement, but they feel as light as a feather. The quality of their movement is very soft and light.

2. This is their time to just enjoy the presence of Jesus and for Him to enjoy their presence. They can use all different levels as they dance with Him, and they can move freely around the room. The focus is to dance freely and lightly, and to enjoy being with Him.

Fourth Phase – approximately three minutes

1. Start playing the fourth track of the instrumental music you have chosen. Preferably something with a slower tempo, but with an adventurous feel to it. Tell the dancers Jesus is taking hold of their hand again. He is gently pulling them toward the ground, and they land on top of a high mountain. This time their movement needs to be very intentional, focused, and controlled because they are at such a high altitude. They have to be specific with their steps. For example, they can imagine stepping over or going around rocks. They are in a very high place, but it's not scary because Jesus is with them. He continues moving and dancing with them.

2. Ask the dancers to pause for a moment. They are in such a high place that they have a great view and can see from Heaven's perspective. They can ask Jesus to show them the view He has for them — something encouraging He wants to show them personally. They can receive this "view" as a literal picture/vision or it can be a word of encouragement. They can continue dancing as they are asking Jesus what the "view" is for them.

Fifth Phase – approximately three minutes

1. Start playing the fifth track of the instrumental music you have chosen. Preferably something slow and soft. Tell the dancers Jesus is taking hold of their hand again. They are coming down from the mountaintop and arrive in a beautiful valley. A garden has been prepared just for them. They can move and dance around the garden, and explore what Jesus has prepared for them. This time their movement is not restricted by anything so their movement is very free and relaxed.

2. Jesus is taking hold of their hand again. He is showing them a secret place to rest that He has prepared for them in the garden. They can sit or lie down in this resting place. They can close their eyes as Jesus is blessing their feet and anointing their head with oil. As the leader, you can walk around the room and lay your hands on their feet or forehead.

Ending:

Tell the dancers Jesus is picking them up and carrying them back to the classroom, dance studio, or wherever you are at. They can slowly open their eyes and sit up. Jesus is still right there with them.

Debrief:

Give the dancers an opportunity to share about their experience. They can do this in pairs and, if you have more time, you can ask if anyone would like to share about this encounter time with the whole group. They can share what kind of gift they received at the bottom of the ocean or what kind of view Jesus showed them on the mountaintop. Or they can share which one of those five places was the most significant for them, or where they felt the most comfortable or the most challenged.

My comments on this exercise:

As I mentioned at the beginning, I created this exercise to help dancers exercise their spiritual senses and to discover different ways of how God can speak and minister to them. I find many people struggle with the fear of "making things up" instead of believing they are hearing from God. I like to break this fear off them at the beginning of this exercise. Jesus has promised us that His sheep hear His voice (John 10:27). What is maybe even more important to understand is that God loves to partner with us. He has given us an imagination for a purpose. He loves to work through our sanctified imagination. You have the mind of Christ (1 Corinthians 2:16). I don't mean every thought you have is God's thought, but you can filter your thoughts through the lens of His love. You can tell the participants that if they feel like they can't hear God, they have the freedom to "make up" the answers for the questions asked throughout this exercise. God loves it when we use our imagination with Him.

The love languages mentioned in this exercise are in the order I presented them in the beginning: 1) The beach – physical touch, 2) The ocean – receiving gifts, 3) The sky – quality time, 4) The mountaintop – words of affirmation, 5) The garden – acts of service. It was on the beach where Jesus first came and took hold of their hand and started initiating the dance through touch. It was in the ocean where God gave them a gift. They spent quality time with Jesus in the sky. The mountaintop was the place where they received words of affirmation, either in the form of a picture or words. In the garden, Jesus came to serve them by preparing them a place to rest, anointing their head with oil, and blessing their feet. I don't always tell the dancers about these different love languages until afterward. I have noticed people often find the love language that is their most prominent way to receive love was expressed in the place where they felt the most comfortable during this exercise. Clearly there can be other factors that make them enjoy one of these places of encounter more than others, like the type of music you play, etc.

In addition to learning to recognize God's presence in different ways, one of the benefits of this exercise is it helps people find different dynamics and texture in their movement. When they imagine being in different environments, their movement quality automatically changes and adapts to it. This exercise is great for helping people step out of their usual way of moving and grow creatively.

Core Value II
Partnership with One Another —
Connection and Community

If we want to build dance communities that are functional, we need to be connected with one another. Dancers need to know the dance community is a safe place to be real, honest, and vulnerable with one another. We need to be able to lean on one another without fear. As dancers this can mean quite literally leaning on one another as we dance and minister together, but we also need to be able to lean on one another figuratively — pulling strength from one another and being there for one another. Vulnerability means we are not only transparent and open with others, but we invite them to give us feedback and welcome them to speak into our lives. This can feel risky because when you allow others in, they have the potential to hurt or disappoint you. However, letting people in is the only way to build real connection, and the benefits of living in community typically far outweigh the risks.

I'm not saying you need to discuss everything that's going on in your heart and your world with all the other dancers (although ideally everyone would have someone in their lives who has this level of access to their heart, which should be your spouse if you are married). However, we need to be building the kind of environment where dancers feel safe to share if they need support from others around them. It's important to not only share struggles, but to also celebrate each other's victories. The level of vulnerability people feel safe with will be determined by the level of trust we have for one another. The only way to build trust is to cultivate relationships that are real with one another. If the only common factor between us is that we do ministry together, our level of connection ends up being quite shallow. Paul set a good example for us in his letter to Thessalonians: *"Because we loved you so much, we were delighted to share with you not only the gospel of God but our lives as well"* (1 Thessalonians 2:8).

Building Connection

Building connection takes time and effort from everyone in the dance community, but it's definitely worth it. We can't force anyone to be vulnerable with others, but we can actively welcome people into the place of connectedness we cultivate and into being part of a family. When I teach my weekly classes for the worship dancers in BSSM, I purposely take time to ask the dancers how they are doing — if they have testimonies or prayer needs they would like to share. I recommend doing this while sitting down in a circle. Facing one another and having eye contact with everyone helps create openness in the atmosphere and makes it easier for people to connect. Of course we can't use the whole class time for just sharing, but I have experienced, in such a tangible way, the blessings that come from taking time for building a real connection. When the students have an opportunity to share and come alongside one other, ministering with each other becomes much easier.

The Bible exhorts us to *"Carry each other's burdens, and in this way you will fulfill the law of Christ"* (Galatians 6:2). The purpose of my weekly class is definitely not to be a counseling session, but it often doesn't require a lot of time to come alongside people and help carry their burdens. We always try to keep the main emphasis on what God is doing instead of focusing on what hasn't happened yet, because whatever we focus on grows. We don't want to magnify problems, but we do want to be aware of the challenges people are facing so we can partner with them in prayer and be part of their breakthrough. I believe God intentionally releases some of our breakthroughs through other people so we don't become too independent. We are created to need each other.

The possibilities for how to do this are numerous, and situations can arise where we need to take more time to minister to one another. As a practical example, I meet with all the dancers from BSSM once a week and lead what is called a dance community class. It's not a dance technique class; the main purpose is rather to build community and connection between the dancers. If my class is one hour long, which it typically is, I spend about the first ten minutes giving the students an opportunity to share what's going on in their lives. I often encourage the students to stretch while we are chatting. We always take time later in the meeting to minister to those students who need some prayer covering, but it doesn't look like a traditional prayer meeting. We do the ministry in various creative ways. For example, one way is to have the students who need ministry sit in the middle of the room, while the other students dance around them, expressing their prayers through dance. We often use big silk scarves while dancing over people. Sometimes using props makes people feel more relaxed, and props can become an extension of their movement. However, I don't want people to hide behind props and use them as "safety blankets," so at times I also purposely ask my students to not use any props.

Since the BSSM dance teams are primarily built for ministering in our school's corporate worship times, I also take some time to process with the students what's going on in their class. This is a great way to help them become more aware of corporate atmospheres and discerning what God is doing in their class. I like to ask them questions in order to help them articulate what they are sensing. Some examples are: What do you feel like God is doing in your class right now? Have there been any themes repeated in the teaching times in your class? What are some of the topics the students have been discussing during break times? You can develop your own questions to suit the environment you're in and to help your students process what God's doing.

At the beginning of the class, we often find the same theme repeats itself when the students share what is going on in their personal lives. What they initially thought was a personal battle or victory often turns out to be happening in the lives of several of the students. This helps us to know how we can pray for the whole school as a community and partner with God, whether it's releasing breakthrough or blessing what God is already doing. We pray into these themes by using dance and movement as our prayer language. A majority of the class time actually tends to be intercession. We always intercede from the place of victory we have in Jesus, releasing the reality of Heaven into every circumstance. Praying and interceding together through dance is one of the most powerful ways of building connection and unity amongst the dancers.

In the BSSM dance community classes we also do different creative movement exercises. Many of these exercises are designed to help the students not only move from the place of a heart to heart connection with God, but to foster connection with one another as a team. Our goal is not to make everyone look the same or dance in the same way or style. We want to call out the unique expression from every dancer and help them find new ways of expressing what God has already placed inside of them. We then move together as a team from a place where we can be each other's biggest champions. You can find some examples of these types of exercises at the end of this chapter.

I realize different settings exist for dance ministries, and it may not be practical for everyone to have the connection and community time during dance classes, especially if your studio time is limited. I encourage you to find ways of helping the dancers connect with one another, not only by dancing together, but by sharing their lives together as well. This could happen in more of a home group setting or whatever works best for your team. Connection within a team takes time, like all relationships do, but it's well worth the time and the effort!

Exercise 4. Calling Out the Gold

When we minister together, it's good to start recognizing the different anointings and giftings that God has blessed each dancer with. Everyone has a unique flavor they carry in their movement. This exercise is designed to call out the treasures we see in one another and the specific things we see people release as they dance. Some of these things seem so obvious that it may feel silly to point them out, but often what you see in others may not be so evident to them. Even if they can see it, it's always good to receive affirmation from people around us. We want to give the dancers permission to be who they are and to welcome the unique flavor they carry into our community and family.

Arrangements:

Have the dancers stand in a big circle. Turn on some instrumental music. Keep the volume down, allowing you to easily speak over the music.

First Phase:

Ask the dancers to hold each other's hands while standing in the circle. *Invite the Holy Spirit to come, manifest His presence, and open everyone's eyes to see what each dancer carries and releases.*

Second Phase:

The dancers can let go of the hands they were holding. One dancer at a time goes and dances in the middle of the circle. The dancer can dance in any dance style they want to. Encourage them to just be themselves and express their heart to God. While one dancer dances, the other dancers call out different words that describe what they see the dancer is releasing with their movement. It is important for these words to be encouraging. Keep the words short, just one or two words at a time. We call them "popcorn" style words. Some examples include: strength, beauty, grace, and breakthrough. Each dancer can take about 20-30 seconds to dance. You don't need to time this — the transition usually happens naturally after everyone has called out a word or two. When one dancer finishes, whoever feels like going next can start dancing. This continues until everyone has had a chance to dance and hear what the others see in their dance.

Debrief:

Ask a couple of dancers to share how it felt for them when others were calling out what they saw them release.

My comments on this exercise:

This exercise is great for releasing identity to the dancers. It helps them recognize what they carry in their dance. It's also a great eye opener for the entire team to see what the others on the team carry. One of the goals is to help the dancers see others and their dance from God's point of view. That's why, even if you have a bigger group of dancers, I recommend doing this exercise in one big circle rather than splitting into smaller groups. This way everyone can hear what each dancer releases and they get to know each other from God's perspective.

Exercise 5. Responding and Affirming

Arrangements:

Have the dancers form groups of four dancers. Have one of the dancers stand in the middle of each group with the other three around them. Each dancer should be about two arms' length away from each other. Choose some instrumental music.

First Phase – approximately one minute

Ask the dancer in the middle of each group to ask God for one specific word describing how He sees her/him. Have that dancer dance out this word, expressing their identity in God.

Second Phase – approximately one minute

Ask the three dancers around the first dancer to respond to what they saw or felt in this dance. Have them respond by dancing around the first dancer, expressing the emotion they felt as she/he was dancing, and reflecting and affirming by their dance what they saw in the first dancer.

Rotate the dancers until everyone has been in the middle, repeating the First and the Second Phase.

Debrief:

Ask the dancers to share, within their groups, the words they received from God for themselves. Ask them to also share how it made them feel when they saw the other dancers respond to their dance.

My comments on this exercise:

This exercise is very simple but powerful. Something very significant happens when we intentionally dance from the place of who God says we are. I have seen many dancers deeply moved and affirmed by seeing how other dancers respond to their own dance, and reflect back to them what God sees in them.

Exercise 6. Mirroring

Dancers start naturally pulling movements from each other's movement vocabulary just by dancing together. The goal is not that we all dance the same way and have the same dance style, but we can always learn from one another. This exercise is great for helping the dancers to come out of their familiar movement pathways and to receive from one another.

Arrangements:

Have the dancers work in duos. Ask them to stand facing one another, approximately two arms' length away from one another so that the dancers' fingertips nearly touch if they both reach out their arms toward each other. Select several different tracks of music, preferably different styles and tempos.

First Phase – approximately two minutes

Ask the dancers to choose which one of the pair will lead first. Turn on the first track of music. As the leader starts moving, the follower who is facing the leader starts copying the leader's movement, like a mirror. If the leader raises her/his right hand, the follower raises her/his left hand. The leader can use all the levels, from lying on the floor to standing on tiptoes or jumping. The leader can move in whatever style she/he wants to. The follower's job is to try to follow so closely and seamlessly that from the outside it would be hard to tell who is leading the movement.

Second Phase – approximately two minutes

Play another track of music of your choice, preferably a different style from the first one. This is the sign for the dancers to change the leaders. They stay with the same partner, but the one who was previously following is now leading.

Third Phase – approximately two minutes

Change the music again. You can either have them keep the same partners and continue alternating leaders, or you can ask the dancers to find another partner each time

you change the music. You can repeat this as many times
as you want.

Fourth Phase – approximately two minutes

Change the music again. Have the dancers stay paired
up, but this time have one of them stand behind the other
dancer, facing their back, and standing approximately
one arm's length away. The dancer who is in front is
leading and the one behind them is following. This time
the dancer who leads does traveling movement, and the
dancer who is behind them copies the movement, following behind them. The leader can freely travel around the
room and use different levels.

Fifth Phase – approximately two minutes

Change the music again. Ask the dancers to turn around,
staying with the same partner. As they turn around, the
follower becomes the leader. Continue doing traveling
movement, like in Phase Four.

Sixth Phase – approximately two minutes

Repeat the Fifth Phase, but this time the leader can join
in with another pair of dancers, while still leading the
follower. For example, if one leader decides to go behind
another pair of dancers, there will be a line of four dancers doing the same travel movement. If another leader
decides to go behind the line of four dancers, it becomes
a line of six dancers, etc.

Debrief:

> Give the dancers an opportunity to share what they felt while dancing.

Exercise 7. Follow the Leader – Diamond and Circle

This exercise is great for helping dancers learn to move in unison. There are times when I have the dancers in BSSM dance together as a group during the corporate worship times at school. Exercises like this are great for helping them to become more comfortable with moving together, learning each other's "movement language," and following one another's movement. It's also a way to teach the dancers how to invite others into their secret place and their own unique journey of encountering God through dance. I see it as an impartation from one dancer to the other dancers of the different flavors of anointing they each carry.

Arrangements:

> Find some slow, instrumental music. Have the dancers get into groups of four and stand in the shape of a diamond. The points of the diamond should correspond to the four walls of the room. Have the dancers stand about two arms' length away from the closest person in their group. Everyone in the group of four is facing the same direction, toward one of the four walls.

First Phase – approximately ten minutes

Turn on some slow tempo music. In each group, the dancer who stands at the front point of the diamond shape (in the direction the group of four dancers is facing) is the first leader. The leader can start moving slowly, and everyone in the group of four follows the leader and copies their movements. Keep the movements slow enough for everyone to follow, with the group of four staying in the shape of a diamond in relation to one another. The leader can use different levels, but while she/he is leading, only one direction can be faced. The leader must continue to face toward the wall she/he was facing when the exercise began. The leader can choose to pass on the leader role to someone else in the group of four by turning toward another wall. Whoever becomes the front point of the diamond shape (closest to the wall everyone is facing), becomes the leader. The leader can choose how long she/he will be leading the movement for the group, and pass on the leader role to someone else whenever she/he wants to. Switching the leaders doesn't need to happen in any particular order — the leader can choose to turn toward any of the other three walls. Try making the transitions so smooth that, from the outside, it's hard to tell when the leader actually changes. Make sure everyone in the group gets a chance to lead.

Second Phase – approximately ten minutes

Keep the music playing. Have all the dancers come into a big circle, with everyone facing the same wall (preferably the wall that has the mirror if you have one). Have the dancers approximately two arms' length away from each other. This time the dancer who is in the front, and closest to the mirror/wall that everyone is facing, is the leader. Everyone should be able to see her/him and follow her/him. This time the leader is not limited by having to only face one direction. The leader can also do movements toward the two front corners (in a diagonal line) or even turn all the way around, as long as she/he makes the turns obvious and moves so slowly that the others can still follow her/him. The movement phrases should always finish toward the front. The leader can also use different levels, but should try to avoid doing a lot of traveling movement so the circle stays quite stationary. When the leader is ready to pass on the leader role, she/he can do a traveling turn or spin toward her/his right. This means everyone in the circle spins in the circle and moves clockwise to the next spot in the circle. The dancer, who was on the left-hand side of the previous leader, now becomes the leader. Rotate the circle until everyone has had a chance to lead. If you have a limited time to do this exercise, you can tell the dancers to lead only a couple of movement phrases, and then pass on the leader role to the next dancer.

Debrief:

Give the dancers an opportunity to share what they felt while dancing. Have them share how it was for them to lead and how it was for them to follow.

Exercise 8. Canons

Canons are another great way to help dancers be connected with one another and work as a team. It's also another tool you can use while having groups of dancers minister in corporate worship settings. You can do canons in many different ways, but this is an example to get you started. This exercise can feel quite technical, but encourage the dancers not to be too serious and to remember to have fun with this. It is a great tool to practice coordination skills and awareness of one another.

Arrangements:

> Have the dancers in groups of four. Have them choose who is number one, who is number two, and so on. Choose several different styles of worship songs to play.

First Phase – approximately five minutes

> Have the dancers stand approximately two arms' length away from each other. They can be in any formation they want to, but ask them to make sure dancer number two can see number one, number three can see number two, and number four can see number three. Turn on some worship music that has distinct eight counts. Dancer number one is leading. The leader does any kind of a short phrase of movement, for example a turn, jump, or slide, for the first two counts of the music and then freezes (pauses and waits in stillness) for the next six counts. Dancer number two does the same movement phrase for the second two counts, and then freezes for the next six counts. Dancer number three does the same for the third

two counts, and then freezes for the next six counts, and dancer number four does the same for the fourth two counts. This can be repeated several times. After a while you can rotate the numbers, so that dancer number one becomes number two, two becomes three, etc.

Second Phase – approximately five minutes

Repeat the First Phase, but this time instead of freezing for six counts, have the dancers improvise by doing slow movements of their own choice during those six counts. If the music is faster, you can give the dancer who starts the canon four counts for the part that gets repeated by the other three dancers. In this case you would use two measures of eight counts for going through the whole canon. Rotate the numbers until everyone has had a turn to be each number.

Third Phase – approximately five minutes

Keep the dancers in groups of four, assigned with numbers from one to four. Start with everyone improvising, doing their own movements. Any time dancer number one does any type of a jump or a turn, number two follows and does the same movement immediately after them (for the next two counts). Number three does the same movement after number two (for the following two counts), and then number four does the same after number three. So this time the dancers only copy the jumps and/or turns, and it's up to dancer number one to decide how often they do a jump or a turn. Rotate the numbers.

Fourth Phase – approximately five minutes

Have the four dancers stand in a single-file line, facing the same direction. Dancer number one is in front and the other three dancers are behind the leader, approximately one arm's length away from each other. This exercise is the easiest to do facing mirrors if you have them. Have number one do any movement for the first two counts, and then freeze for the next six counts, using the same counting pattern as in the First Phase. Dancer number two does the same movement for the following two counts, but this time toward the opposite direction. Thus, if number one does an arm swing to the right, number two would do the same thing to the left. Number three would do it to the right, and then number four would do it to the left. The dancers always go the opposite direction to the dancer in front of them. The leader should always face the front, and her/his movement can go either toward the sides or in a diagonal line toward the front. The leader can use different levels, but each movement phrase should always return into the formation of a line. Rotate the numbers by having the leader go to the back of the line, and everyone taking one step forward.

Debrief:

Give the dancers an opportunity to share what they felt while dancing. Have them share how it was for them to lead and how it was for them to follow.

Exercise 9. Intercessory Group Dance

Arrangements:

Have the dancers form groups of three to six dancers, depending on how many dancers you have. Choose a different instrumental track of music for each group. You can either give each group a topic to intercede for, or ask them to come up with a topic by themselves. The topic shouldn't be more than one or two words. For example, their topic could be unity, confidence, or joyful anticipation.

First Phase – approximately five minutes

Have one group at a time dance their prayer. All the others are sitting down in a big circle around the room and observing. Do not give them time to plan what they will do as a group, but have them do all of it spontaneously, listening to the Holy Spirit and one another. By listening to one another, I mean non-verbal communication. They can use any of the tools from the previous exercises, such as following one another's movements spontaneously or doing canons. Or they can try finding similar dynamics in their movement expression. They can also complement one another's movement expression. An example of this is one dancer dancing to the melody line, and the others responding to the beats and the rhythm of the music. The main goal is that they are expressing this prayer together and connecting with each other in some way.

Debrief:

Ask the dancers who were observing to comment if there were specific parts of the dance that stood out to them or ministered to them, or if there were any moments when they felt a shift in the atmosphere. You can also have them guess what the word was that the group was releasing as they were dancing. Afterward, ask the dancers who just danced if there were any moments that stood out to them and how they felt about the whole experience. Have them share the actual word they danced.

Second Phase – approximately five minutes (per group)

Have the next group come up and dance their word as a prayer, repeating the First Phase. Include the debrief time. Do this with each group.

Third Phase – approximately five minutes (per group)

Repeat the First and the Second Phase, but this time ask the group of dancers to make sure one or two dancers are always moving at floor level. If it's a group of 3-4 dancers, one of them should always be moving on the low level. If it's a group of 5-6 dancers, two of them should always move on the low level. If a dancer who starts on the floor decides to get up, then one of the other dancers should take note of it right away and start moving on the low level. This requires the whole group to be constantly aware of one another's movements and whereabouts.

Debrief:

Debrief after each group has danced. You can use the same questions as after the First Phase.

My comments on this exercise:

This is one of my favorite exercises. The main reason why I love it is that the dancers are always surprised by how powerfully the Holy Spirit moves through their dance. Every time the prayers are expressed in unique and different ways. This exercise is also great for teaching dancers to multitask and to increase their spatial awareness. They learn to fill up the space that needs to be filled. They also learn to be aware of their whole group and to explore the different dynamics at play within the group, such as being able to respond to the other dancers, taking the initiative to lead, and being willing to follow others. Most importantly, they learn to listen to the Holy Spirit while doing all of this. Dancers can grow in all of these areas through practice. Practicing all these different aspects is very important, especially for dance teams that minister together. You can encourage the dancers to continue practicing by reminding them that growth is a process, and they can celebrate their progress throughout their journey.

In this exercise, the debrief time is very helpful and revelatory. The dancers who are observing can see things that the dancers who are dancing may not see themselves. Learning to articulate what we see and hear is also a skill we can develop by practice.

If you have colorful silks or pieces of fabric, you can give the dancers the option of using them in this exercise as well.

Exercise 10. Conversations

Arrangements:

Have the dancers divide into groups of three and stand in the shape of a triangle, about two arms' length away from each other, everyone facing the center. Turn on some music that has distinct eight counts.

First Phase – approximately five minutes

In the groups of three, choose one dancer who will start. This dancer improvises for eight counts and then stops and freezes in front of one of the other two dancers. The second dancer (in front of whom the first dancer freezes) responds to the movement of the first dancer and dances for the next eight counts. The second dancer stops and freezes in front of the third dancer. The third dancer responds to the movement of the second dancer, dancing for the following eight counts. The dance becomes like a conversation between all three dancers. You can repeat this as many times as you want to.

Second Phase – approximately five minutes

Repeat the First Phase, but this time tell the dancers to do most of their movement on the low level, using the floor as much as possible.

Debrief:

Have the dancers share in their groups how the exercise was for them, and if they were able to recognize any themes that came up in their "movement conversation."

My comments on this exercise:

This exercise is great for teaching the dancers to be aware of one another and responding to what is already happening. This requires that everyone lays down their own agendas and is fully tuned into what the other dancers are trying to communicate.

4

Core Value III
Pursuing Excellence

One of the things that makes me feel upset is when people hear the words "dance ministry" and they immediately associate it with dance that's done poorly, at a skill level that is sort of embarrassing. I believe God wants us to be people of excellence in every area. In order to *"make His praise glorious"* (Psalm 66:2), we need to be willing to grow and develop our craft. I always encourage my dancers to take technique classes and push themselves to grow creatively, artistically, and in their dance technique. But excellence is so much more than just developing our skills. We need excellence of heart, excellence of attitude, and excellence in hosting and carrying the presence of God and communicating His heart to others.

I like the definition Wikipedia gives the word excellence: *"Excellence is a talent or quality, which is unusually good and so surpasses ordinary standards"* http://en.wikipedia.org/wiki/ Excellence. As people of God, we are not called to be ordinary, but to surpass all ordinary standards. We are called to live supernatural lives and carry the breath of Heaven in everything we do. The excellence that comes from the presence of God in us should be visible and tangible to people around us.

When looking for dancers for ministry teams, I look for people who have excellence written all over them. They have an excellent attitude; they are teachable and willing to serve a bigger vision than themselves. They are people who are willing to grow in every area — I don't require anyone to be on a professional level in dance technique, but I do want everyone to be willing to grow and develop their skills. They are people who are running hard after God, but I'm not talking about striving or perfectionism. Those are counterfeits of excellence, caused by religion and legalism. True excellence comes from God's presence and from His love. The Bible doesn't actually use the word excellence, but 1 Corinthians introduces the famous chapter on love with the words: *"And now I will show you the most excellent way"* (1 Corinthians 12:31b). This most excellent way is love. Real excellence is always rooted in love. If we want to operate in true excellence, we need to always stay motivated by love. This applies not only while operating in the spiritual gifts, like this passage is referring to, but in every area of our lives.

Displaying excellence in dance ministry

There are many different ways to do, and platforms for, dance ministry. In BSSM we have dance teams that minister outside of church and dance in different neighborhoods in the local community. We have dance teams to activate children in dance at after school programs. We have dance teams that dance at different events and minister to individuals by dancing over them and giving them prophetic words through dance. We have dance teams that dance in the Healing Rooms and release God's presence over people who need either physical or inner healing. We also have dance teams to perform dance pieces specifically choreographed for certain events. And we have dance teams that minister during corporate worship times on stage. I will explore these different types of ministry later on.

I always try to find the best and the most suitable spot for each dancer. This process includes many factors, and some helpful questions to explore include: Where are they at on their personal journey with dance? What type of dance training do they have? What kind of season are they in right now? It's not like all these dance ministries are open for anyone who feels like joining, but I believe a place exists for anyone who has a heart of excellence to serve in some area. For example, not everyone is ready to minister by dancing on stage. We need to learn to be okay with the process. I tend to ask a higher level of technical dance skills from the dancers who minister on stage compared with some other ministry settings. This is not because dancing on stage is more important, but because excellence on stage looks different from excellence in ministering to an individual through dance in a more private setting, and it's different from excellence in activating children in dance. Yet, even if a dancer has a high level of technical skill, but doesn't show any excellence in their commitment level and is not willing to be part of the community, she/he wouldn't be a good fit for a ministry team. The dancer's readiness to be teachable and their commitment and investment in the dance community are some of the foundational virtues, demonstrating excellence of heart and attitude.

For the dance teams that perform choreographed pieces, having technical skill is very crucial. It's wise to do auditions according to the dance style you are planning on choreographing with. I always try to remind the dancers in our dance community that the goal is not for everyone to dance on stage. The goal is to find your specific calling in dance. We are all at our best, most effective, and most happy when we serve in the place God has designed for us, and designed us for. Whatever type of calling you may have in dance, whether it's leading others in corporate worship settings, performing choreographed dance pieces, activating children — or any age group — in dance, doing dance outreach, intercessory dance, all of the above, or something completely different and groundbreaking, it is always a great plan for everyone to take dance technique classes. We want to give our best to God and be known for excellence in every way.

Like I said earlier, excellence is certainly not all about technique. As I have been building the dance community in BSSM, I have kept the main focus on helping the students to grow in excellence in hearing God's voice and in learning to express God's heart through dance. I can't overemphasize how important practicing this in a safe environment is. (If you are interested in reading more about the Biblical foundation for prophetic dance, there's a whole chapter on this topic in *Encountering God Through Dance*.) Just like in other areas, we need to practice moving in the prophetic in order to learn and grow. Here are some examples of the exercises I have been using for the dancers to grow in the prophetic — in hearing God's heart and communicating it.

Exercise 11. Dancing Over People – Prophetic Words

Arrangements:

Find some instrumental music. Have the dancers get into groups of three. Each group chooses who will be the first person to receive ministry. The other two dancers will be the ministry team.

First Phase – approximately five minutes

The dancer who is receiving ministry can either sit down on the floor or stand. Encourage the receiving dancers to keep their eyes open during the ministry time. Many times God speaks to people directly through the dance movements; therefore it's important they see the dance. *Welcome the Holy Spirit to come and speak to everyone.* Turn on some instrumental music, or if you want you can do this exercise in silence as well. The two dancers who are ministering will start dancing around the person who is receiving ministry. They can either dance together or take turns. Encourage them to keep asking the Holy Spirit to lead them and give them some specific words for the receiving dancer while they are dancing. If they want to wait in stillness for a moment and ask God to give them a word before they start dancing, that's okay too, but they don't necessarily need to have a word before they start dancing. Many times God speaks while we are already in motion.

If you have pieces of silk or other fabric, you can have the dancers dance with those as well. Ask them to be intentional about the color of the silk they use. There may be a certain color of fabric they feel drawn to because it's part of the prophetic word they are delivering. For example, a dancer may pick up a red piece of silk to dance with, and the word they give may have to do with God surrounding the receiving dancer with His love. Some books have been written on the Biblical meaning for different colors, but more than anything I would encourage the dancers to ask the Holy Spirit for a personal meaning for each color. Sometimes God can lead you to dance with a certain color of silk just because it happens to be the favorite color of the person you are ministering to.

Debrief:

Fade out the music. First ask the dancers who were receiving to comment on what they saw in the dance, or how they felt as they were receiving ministry. Were there any parts of the dance that specifically spoke to them? After they have shared, have the dancers who were ministering share briefly what they felt God was saying through their movement and if they got any specific words while they were dancing.

Second Phase

Repeat the First Phase including the debrief time two more times, switching the dancer who is receiving until everyone gets a chance to be the receiver.

My comments on this exercise:

I love this exercise because it invites the dancers into a place of hearing God's heart and expressing it. Many times dancers who have believed the lie that they can't hear God's voice are blown away by how powerfully God speaks through their dance! I find it helpful to first demonstrate this exercise, especially if the dancers have never done anything like this before. It's also good to talk through the basic guidelines in prophetic ministry before releasing the dancers to go for it. According to the New Testament, prophecy is meant for *"strengthening, encouragement and comfort"* (1 Corinthians 14:3). We want to release Heaven's perspective into people's lives. At Bethel, we often use the metaphor of "calling out the gold" in people. We are not digging up the dirt in them. We always want to leave people who receive ministry in a better place than where they were before. Even if you would be rightfully discerning that the person you are ministering to is, for example, depressed, it's not very helpful if you give them a word or dance about depression. Instead you should speak or dance the opposite, releasing the joy of the Lord and His glory over them. Ezekiel used this same strategy. He saw a vision of dry bones, and he didn't prophesy what he saw — he prophesied life to those bones (Ezekiel 37).

This particular exercise is something that can be used as a ministry tool in various settings, not only in the classroom. We use this ministry style a lot in the Healing Rooms. Many of our teams have also used this way of ministering in different outreach events. It can be a great tool during any ministry time, whether inside or outside of the church walls. However, if you want to do this type of ministry outside of your own classroom, it's important that you first ask for permission, not only from the leaders of the ministry under whose covering you are serving, but also permission from the person you are ministering to.

Here are some practical guidelines:

Never send dancers to dance over others alone. Have them go in groups of at least two. It's always safer to do ministry with someone else. It's safer for the dancers and safer for the person who is receiving ministry. Be aware of people's personal space. As dancers, we can be quite comfortable being in close proximity with each other, but other people may not be comfortable if you dance closely to them. We want to honor people and help them feel safe to receive from God as we minister. If you choose to use silks or any scarves as you dance, be sensitive in how you use them. Sometimes it may be appropriate to lay a silk on someone's feet or shoulders, but never cover anyone's face — we clearly don't want to suffocate people or frighten them. We also don't want to whack people with the silk, or with anything else for that matter. Some of this may sound extremely obvious, but I have seen several awkward situations in which dancers were "ministering" to people in ways that were inappropriate (even though their hearts were in the right place), and therefore suggest you give clear guidelines to your teams. I personally don't recommend using any flags for dancing over people because the sticks can be unsafe, even if you are being careful. We definitely don't want to poke anyone's eye out. Having said all that, remember to have fun and expect God to move powerfully through you!

Exercise 12. Shifting Atmospheres

Arrangements:

Have the dancers spread out around the classroom. Find some instrumental music.

First Phase – approximately ten minutes

Turn on the music, but keep the volume down so you can speak over the music. Call out one word that has a positive meaning and can be used for describing an atmosphere or a type of anointing in a room (e.g., joy, breakthrough, rest, freedom, peace, healing). Have the dancers respond to the word you call out, releasing the word in the room through their movement. Ask them to dance the feeling of the word, rather than literally representing the word. Call out a new word about every 30 seconds. Ask the dancers to focus on just dancing the words, even if the music you are playing would seemingly carry a different atmosphere.

Second Phase – approximately five minutes

Repeat the First Phase, but have the dancers take turns in spontaneously calling out the words while they are dancing.

Third Phase – approximately five minutes

Turn the music off. Use the same pattern as in the Second Phase, but this time have the dancers take turns in making sounds and responding to those sounds. They can make the different sounds by using their voice, stomping their feet, clapping their hands, snapping their fingers, or through other creative methods they develop. The sounds can be done as frequently as the dancers want to, and the dancers always respond to the latest sound they heard.

Debrief:

Give the dancers an opportunity to share how they felt during this exercise. Ask them if they could feel the atmosphere change with everyone dancing to the same word or the same sound.

My comments on this exercise:

This exercise is great for teaching the dancers that they don't always need to focus on just moving with the music, but they can tune into responding to other stimuli as well. This exercise also demonstrates how our movement can literally shift the atmosphere in the room. Learning the skill of responding to words and sounds helps us flow with the Holy Spirit while we dance in any environment. Whenever we hear God whispering a word to us, we can focus on releasing that word.

Exercise 13. Personal Prophetic Intercession

Arrangements:

Have the dancers spread out throughout the classroom. Choose three different tracks of instrumental music.

First Phase – approximately five minutes

Turn on the first track of music. Ask the dancers to start interceding through dance for the next month ahead of them. If they have a certain area in their lives where they want to see a breakthrough in the following month, they can start by praying for that. For example, they may want breakthrough in finances or relationships, and they can begin there. Ask them to remain open to the Holy Spirit, and to listen if He wants to speak to them about a different topic than they had initially thought of. The dancers can start dancing right away, even if they don't know what they are praying for at the beginning. As mentioned earlier, God often speaks to us once we are already in motion. The dancers can intercede through their movement for several things, but ask them to narrow it down to one topic, and preferably narrow it down even further to just one or two words.

Second Phase – approximately five minutes

Play a different music track. Ask the dancers to do a prayer dance for the next month. If the first month they interceded for was January, they will now be praying for February. Follow the same guidelines as in the First Phase.

Third Phase – approximately five minutes

Play a different track of music. Ask the dancers to do a prayer dance for the subsequent month. If the last month they interceded for was February, they will now be praying for March. Follow the same guidelines as in the First Phase.

Debrief:

Ask the dancers to write down the three topics/areas for which they interceded for the next three months. It's a good thing to have them write it all down so they won't forget, and so they can give thanks to God for the breakthroughs as they see them coming. Ask if anyone wants to share their experience, or what they interceded for, with the others. Ask if anyone felt like God spoke to them about something different from what they originally thought of praying for.

My comments on this exercise:

This exercise is great for training the dancers for prophetic intercession. It teaches the students how intercession and the prophetic go hand in hand. Many times the dancers are surprised by what God speaks to them while they are in a place of prayer and intercession.

Exercise 14. Prophetic Intercession for the Nations

Arrangements:

> Tell the dancers the classroom floor represents the world map. Show them in which direction are north, south, east, and west. Show them where on the floor you see each continent located. Find some worship music.

First Phase – approximately five minutes

> *Invite the Holy Spirit to lead this prayer time.* Turn on the music. Tell the dancers they can start with any continent or country they have a heart for. Invite them to start dancing over the continent or country, releasing God's presence in that region. They are free to go and dance over multiple countries, or even do a tour around the world. Ask them to keep their hearts open, and to follow if the Holy Spirit leads them to pray over a country or region they hadn't thought of before. If you have silks, you can give them the option of using them while they dance.

Second Phase – approximately five minutes

> Ask the dancers to ask the Holy Spirit to show them something specific in one country to pray for while they dance. For instance, they may feel led to pray for the economical or political situation, or for the leaders or the president of a certain country. They can also ask the Holy Spirit to show them even more specific things, such as the face of a child who needs prayer right now in that country.

Debrief:

> Ask if any dancers want to share what God showed them or what their experience was like. Give the dancers a few moments to write down some key things they saw, heard, or felt while they were dancing.

My comments on this exercise:

> I often meet dancers who find traditional prayer meetings very challenging and become easily distracted. This exercise has helped many of them gain a bigger heart for prayer and intercession. Dancing not only helps them to stay focused, but they also have experienced God speaking to them in powerful ways while they dance their prayers. Of course we should also use words when we pray, but movement is like another language that helps us in our communication with God.

Exercise 15. Interpreting "Tongues"

At times, I intentionally pray some specific prayers to God through dance. Other times when I dance in God's presence, my spirit is very connected with Him, but I don't necessarily know what I'm praying for. It's like a Heavenly language that I speak with my body — like speaking in tongues.

I have heard that the gift of interpreting tongues is one of the least actively used gifts of the Holy Spirit in the modern day church, but I suggest we actually use (or at least could potentially use) this gift a lot through the arts. I would love to see the church as a whole being more activated in this gift. That's why I love doing exercises where we practice "interpreting tongues" by interpreting dance as an expression and a language of God's heart. *Please note this is not intended as a comment on whether or not we should use the gift of interpreting spoken tongues in public meetings.*

Arrangements:

Have the dancers get into groups of six. Split each group of six into two groups of three dancers. Have these two groups of three face each other. They can stand in a line or any formation they choose. Find some instrumental music.

First Phase – approximately five minutes

Ask each group to choose which half of the group will dance first. The three who are not dancing will be observing the other three dancers who are dancing. *Invite the Holy Spirit to speak through the dance.* Turn on some instrumental music. The first three dancers in each group can start dancing. Ask them to intentionally partner with the Holy Spirit and with one another as they dance in front of the other three dancers in their group. Partnering in this context can look different from group to group. The dancers can do contact improvisation by having moments of physical touch with each other. If it feels like one of the dancers is tapping into something significant with her/his movement, the other two can start following and doing the same movement together. You can also let them know they can do still poses in the midst of the movement, but most importantly encourage them to listen to the Holy Spirit and let Him lead their dance.

Second Phase – approximately five minutes

Ask the dancers who were observing each group to share (within their groups of six) what they saw in the dance and what God spoke to them through it.

Third Phase – approximately five minutes

Swap roles. The three dancers who were observing will now dance, and the ones who were previously dancing will observe.

Fourth Phase – approximately five minutes

Repeat the Second Phase.

Debrief:

Have everyone come together into a big circle. Ask a couple of people to share about their experiences, both in dancing and in interpreting.

My comments on this exercise:

I love seeing dancers surprised by how clearly God speaks through their dance when they intentionally partner with Him. I also love how this exercise demonstrates how God speaks through community — within each group, every dancer plays a part in the bigger picture.

For some dancers it may feel easier to first ask God for a specific word and then dance it, while other dancers may find it easier to first "dance in tongues" and interpret the word afterward (or have others interpret it). It's great to practice and learn to operate in both ways.

5

Core Value IV
Pastoral Covering

Pastoral covering is an integral part of building dance ministries. As I mentioned in the first chapter, the lack of covering can easily take ministries off track. Covering is never meant to be there for the sake of control or limitation. Just like in gardening, the covering over the seeds that have been planted is never there to choke the plants, but to protect them, allowing the plants to grow in a healthy way and become all they were intended and created to be. Worship dancers are in many ways on the front lines of battle, and therefore need to be spiritually covered and protected. It's a very vulnerable thing to hold nothing back and pour your heart out to the Lord in front of other people. This is one reason why it's important to create a safe environment for every dancer who ministers.

As a pastor for the dance teams in BSSM, I need to make sure the dancers are absorbing and embracing our core values before sending them out to minister. I touched on this topic in the previous chapter, but it's significant enough to revisit. It's not necessarily everyone's calling to be leading others in worship through dance, but as a pastor you want to find places where everyone can be activated in one way or another. Of course we are not expecting anyone to be perfect; if that was the case, only Jesus could do dance ministry! However, it is good to use your discernment to see if each dancer is emotionally, spiritually, and physically in a place that is safe to minister. This is primarily for the protection of the dancer, and additionally protects the people they are ministering to. In a corporate worship setting, we want to make sure the dancers won't become a distraction for the people in the congregation. As stated previously, we are not expecting perfection, but we do expect our dancers to be teachable and have hearts that are after God. Connection and community with the dancers helps us remain aware of where they are at, and helps keep their hearts in a healthy place.

As a pastor, I want to be accessible to the dancers. Several of my dancers don't feel comfortable sharing much about their personal lives in a group setting, but they are more than ready to open up when I meet with them one on one. Some of them can be in urgent need of prayer and/or encouragement, so I always save some slots in my calendar for meetings with my students. I'm not a trained counselor and, to be frank, counseling is not at all the purpose of these meetings. If any of my students seem to need some professional help, I would refer them to someone else. The students don't need to be having a crisis in order to meet with me, I just love hearing their stories and getting to know them better. In most cases, my meetings with the dancers are about building connection, listening to them, and encouraging them on their journey. This is not a small thing. Oftentimes all it takes for people to get break-through and go to a higher level is having someone believe in them. In my experience, creatively wired people, like dancers, are especially in need of spiritual mothers and fathers who believe in them.

Pastoring the room and protecting the corporate atmo-sphere

As a dance pastor, I don't only pastor my dancers, but I do my part in pastoring the whole room during the corporate worship sets. In our environment, we don't let just anyone randomly dance on stage, in the same way that we don't let anyone randomly start playing an instrument on stage. This may sound obvious, but unfortunately it's not always apparent to everyone. As a dance pastor, I take responsibility for pas-toring the entire room, creating a safe environment, protect-ing what the Holy Spirit is doing in the room, and covering the dancers. Within our school setting, there may be moments when we open the dance area for anyone who wants to, but this is only for specific times of helping people step into their personal breakthroughs and overcoming their fears.

When my dance teams minister at school, the goal is not their personal breakthrough or freedom. They will receive that as well, but the focus is completely different. I'm teach-ing them to partner with the Holy Spirit and the worship team in releasing God's heart in that specific moment for that particular group. We are focused on what God is doing corporately, rather than looking for our own breakthroughs. The dance team is under my pastoral covering, and they are dancers who are committed to live in connection with one another and grow together.

I have had situations when a random person who I don't know has jumped on stage to dance. This is not something that happens frequently, but as a dance pastor I need to be ready to handle these situations. One day a young lady ran up on stage and started dancing. I don't think she was intentionally trying to do anything wrong, but she definitely wasn't part of the team, and the clothes she wore were very much not dance appropriate according to our guidelines (you can see our dress code at the end of this chapter). I didn't want to embarrass her, but I also didn't want her to interrupt the whole worship set. I went on stage myself and, by gently taking hold of her hand, I literally danced her off the stage. I did it so discretely that I don't think many people even noticed I came to pull her off the stage. Afterward, I had a chat with her backstage. I wanted to celebrate her taking a risk, but also communicated this wasn't an appropriate time for it. I explained how our dance ministry teams work and invited her to come and join our dance community classes if she was interested in being part of the ministry. When situations like this happen, it's very important to keep your love on and make people feel valued and honored, even if you need to bring correction.

There can also be moments when it is very appropriate to lead the whole room into some corporate expression of worship through dance. If this were something my dancers and I wanted to initiate, I would first discuss this with the leader who is overseeing the meeting, as well as check with the worship leader. However, these moments often happen spontaneously, and the worship leader or the leader of the meeting may invite the dance teams to help activate the entire room in dance in the middle of the worship meeting. We have had some outrageously fun times doing this! We always want to honor our leaders and be willing to set aside our plans if the Holy Spirit is changing the direction of the meeting.

Pastoring the dancers in corporate worship times

One of the most important ways we can extend covering over the dancers is by praying for them. We model the importance of prayer covering in every worship setting we dance in. I always have the dancers arrive early enough to warm up and stretch, and to connect with one another and pray before worship starts. As a pastor, I want to create an environment where the dancers feel safe to share if they need any specific prayer before ministering in worship. I ask them questions to check that they are feeling well physically, emotionally, and spiritually before sending them out to dance. For BSSM worship sets, I only ask the students to be there 15 minutes before worship starts because worship is in the middle of their school day. Ideally I would have the team meet at least thirty minutes before the service starts. Our church dance ministry teams meet an hour before the meeting, and that has worked really well for us. If possible, we also try finding time to pray with the worship leaders and musicians. If we have other visual artists ministering with us, I love including them in our prayer times as well.

As a pastor, I'm guiding and leading the whole dance team through the worship set. I'm tuning my heart to listen to what's going on corporately in that particular meeting and what's on God's heart for all of us. I navigate through the process of discerning what it looks like in practical terms for our team to partner with Heaven, the musicians, and the whole worship team. I prayerfully consider when it's a good moment to send a dancer or two to minister, and who to send. I also welcome my team into this journey of listening and hearing from God, and discerning how to apply what we are hearing in the meeting. I want to teach and coach my dancers in this process and help them understand we all can hear from God and grow in our discernment.

As the team shares what God is showing them, it is important that someone has the final say on what the dancers will
actually do in practical terms, providing clarity rather than
confusion. This is true especially if the dancers are sensing
various things. This is why it's crucial to have a pastor/leader
as a point person for the team. When first starting out, gener-
ally speaking, it's wise for the person who is pastoring the
dance team to have this role, but it's helpful to mentor others
in leading the team as well. Once this happens, the dance pastor no longer needs to be leading the team in every meeting.
This also creates room for growth into leadership positions
for the dancers. As you are training new leaders for dance
teams, you want to help them grow in their discernment, but
at the end of the day it's not so much about hearing accurately
or even making the right decisions. It's more about maintain-
ing their heart to heart connection with God, moving from a
place of love, and bringing clarity and direction to what the
dancers are doing. When it comes to deciding who goes to
dance and when, it's not really a question of right or wrong.
It's more about us going on this adventure with God, partnering with Him, and creating with Him. Every leader adds their
own flavor to this journey. I'm convinced God loves everyone's worship to Him at all times. Having said that, we do
want to learn to be sensitive to the Holy Spirit and find those
moments when it's most helpful for the corporate atmosphere
to send out a dancer/dancers.

It's also good for the dancers to learn how the anointing flows
through the leadership. I'm part of the dance team for Bethel
conferences, and have had several experiences when my leader has asked me to dance, and I didn't necessarily feel like
dancing at that specific time. But as I stepped out in faith, I
experienced God's presence in a powerful way. Remember,
the main goal is to partner with God's heart. Often we can

discern what God is doing by feeling atmospheres or seeing in the Spirit, but it's important we don't mix that up with our own personal feelings. There may be moments when the dancers don't necessarily feel like dancing, but the band is leading the room into a place of celebration and freedom, so we choose to dance anyway. As a pastor, I do want to be sensitive to my dancers and never force anyone to dance if they absolutely don't want to. I do, however, expect the dancers on the team to be willing to dance, and if someone is constantly not willing or ready, it would be good to find out why and reconsider if they should be on the team.

Partnering with the musicians

We always aim to partner in leading the room in the direction the musicians and worship leaders are heading. I love being able to connect with the worship leaders beforehand to ask if they have sensed any specific themes God is showing them for this particular worship set. Throughout all worship sets, we intentionally look for ways to support and undergird the worship teams. As a pastor, I want to make sure the worship leaders know that the dancers' hearts are with them and for them. We let them lead, and we follow them. I frequently tell my dancers to not only pray for the dance team, but to also be praying for the musicians and the whole worship team throughout the worship set. In a sense, I see the dance teams as the intercessory troops, both on stage and off stage.

As we build trust with the worship teams and partner with them, there can be times when the dancers get to lead the worship team, and the musicians actually start following the dancers. I have experienced this multiple times in the Healing Rooms and in BSSM, but we never want to force this to happen. We position ourselves to be there to serve the worship band and to support them. This is especially important if you have new worship leaders or guest worship leaders.

In both BSSM and the Healing Rooms, we have built so much trust with the worship teams that they have given me, as a dance pastor, permission to do pretty much anything I feel the Holy Spirit is leading us to do. This gives us a lot of freedom in our practical applications to release God's heart to the corporate atmosphere through dance. We even have a good deal of freedom when deciding where on the stage to dance. We don't want to abuse our freedom, but to be sensitive to the Holy Spirit and to the rest of the worship team. We also don't want to overdo things, and less is often more. (I talk more on this subject in *Encountering God Through Dance*.) In BSSM, I usually have the dance teams ministering on one side of the stage. I have the freedom to have the dancers in front of the worship band, or even behind them or around them, but I do this only in the moments when it really feels appropriate. I wouldn't send the dancers to dance in front or around a guest worship team unless I had first checked if they are okay with it.

Practical ways to extend covering over dancers in worship

Part of covering the dancers is to pray for them while they dance as well as afterward. I usually have between three to six dancers scheduled for the worship sets when we are dancing, and I typically have one to three dancers ministering on stage at a time. There are moments when I may have the entire team dance together, but these moments are rare, and specifically for times when it feels like more dancers are needed for a corporate breakthrough. There isn't a formula to determine the number of dancers who should be ministering at any given moment, but most of the time we have limited space on stage and having only a couple of dancers at a time is most practical. We also don't want to overpower the meetings with too much movement and become a distraction. There may be times when it is very appropriate to have a huge dance party with everyone dancing, but we need to be sensitive to the Holy Spirit and partner with Him and the worship team. In our corporate worship settings, this tends to be easier with just a few dancers.

While one or two of the dancers are dancing, the others are praying for those who are ministering. When I'm leading the dance team, I usually kneel in a corner of the stage to pray for the dancers while they are ministering on stage, being sure to kneel where they can see me. This is one of the ways to help create as safe of an environment as possible for the dancers. This physical presence on stage helps them feel, and remember they are, covered spiritually. It's also important that I can have eye contact with the dancers while they are ministering. This way I can communicate with them and give them signals if needed.

I have developed a couple of subtle hand motions to communicate transition times. If I'm keeping my hands up, with my palms toward them, it's a signal that I'm just blessing them and they should keep on dancing. However, I do tell my dancers they can come off the stage any time they feel they are finished. If I take my hands slowly down and keep my palms toward the floor, it's a signal that I feel like the dancers should slow down and kneel or sit on the floor, and just wait in stillness for a moment. If I turn the palms of my hands toward myself, motioning slowly with my fingers, it's a signal for them to start transitioning off the stage. I do these signals in such a discrete way that no one else, except the dancers, usually even notices I'm doing it. I don't always need to use these signals because the dancers start sensing the moments of transition on their own, but, especially in the beginning, it's good to have some means of communication between the leader and the dancers so everyone feels safe.

During the actual worship time, we avoid too much verbal processing because we want to be tuning into what's going on in the room. When the dancers have finished their dancing, we immediately gather around them to lay hands on them and bless them. Most of the time my dancers feel great afterward. On rare occasions, a dancer may feel something negative, but if they picked up anything negative or peculiar in the atmosphere, we simply "brush them off" by praying for them. Even if everyone is feeling good, it's always a good idea to bless the dancers and seal the words they just released in the room. This is not a time for long prayers — we simply lay hands on the dancers who have just been ministering and cover them through prayer. After the worship set is over, we meet to debrief and to check that everyone is feeling good. I usually give the dancers an opportunity to briefly share what they felt during the worship. Even if we only have a short time for this, it's important to release a blessing over the dancers before they go.

Tuning our hearts to listen

I shared a few exercises in previous chapters that are helpful for training the dancers to dance from the position of a heart to heart connection with God and to be sensitive to the Holy Spirit and to each other while ministering together. The more the dancers do these types of exercises together, the easier it becomes to flow spontaneously together. I absolutely love the times when following one another, doing canons, etc. just happens without any verbal communication, but there may be times when verbal communication is needed. For example, at times I feel like we should be releasing unity in the room, and I ask all the dancers to come up at the same time and follow my movements. Or I may select a dancer to lead everyone in unison. However, the ultimate goal is to help the dancers stay in a place where they are continuously listening to the Holy Spirit and responding to Him, and not merely acting like puppets that only do what the dance team leader asks them to do. Here is an exercise to help the dancers discern for themselves the timing to start and finish their dance.

Exercise 16. Listening for the Timing

Arrangements:

Choose some tracks of various worship songs. Have the dancers sit in a big circle in the dance studio or classroom. You can have a pile of different colored silks in the middle of the classroom.

First Phase – approximately 15 minutes

Tell the dancers you will be playing different worship songs for about 15 minutes. They get to use their own discernment and ask the Holy Spirit when it is their time to go and dance in the middle of the circle, and when it is their time to stop dancing. It doesn't matter if only one dancer is dancing, or if many dancers are dancing at the same time. If someone else is already dancing when a new dancer joins in, they are encouraged to partner with each other, and be aware of what's happening in the big picture. Nobody is doing just their own thing — they are all adding their part to the picture. They don't necessarily need to dance in a similar style or do the same movements, but encourage them to explore different ways of partnering with others. For example, they can create similar texture in their movements, or complement each other's expression by purposefully moving at varying speeds and using different levels in their dance. You can also have the dancers ask the Holy Spirit to give them a specific word to release. After they feel like they have released the word, they can go back into the circle of dancers. The dancers can also ask the Holy Spirit if a certain color of silk reflects the word they are releasing, and they can dance with that silk.

Second Phase – approximately 15 minutes

Repeat the First Phase, but tell the dancers they can now initiate bringing in other dancers to dance with them. They can do this by simply walking to another dancer in the circle, reaching their hand toward them, and helping them up. Each dancer decides how long she/he will dance. If a dancer is invited to dance by another dancer, it's still up to her/him to ask the Holy Spirit how long to dance.

Debrief:

Give the dancers a chance to share how they felt about this exercise. Ask them if they got any specific words they were releasing.

My comments on this exercise:

This exercise is great for teaching the dancers to listen to the Holy Spirit for specific timing and to look for key moments when they fit in. It also helps them to be intentional about what they release as they dance. The Second Phase helps them to grow in leading others, and to actively listen to the Holy Spirit not only for themselves, but for other dancers as well.

Dress Code

An area you will need to navigate through in pastoring dancers is inevitably the dress code for dancing. I am often asked if we have a specific dress code for the worship dancers. I like rephrasing this question: How can we best serve and honor people and God by what we wear? There are definitely various cultural approaches when it comes to dance clothes. Different church cultures exist, even within the same country. I talk more about this subject in my book *Encountering God Through Dance*.

In our church culture, a high level of freedom exists for people to express themselves through different styles of clothes and to be uniquely themselves. For the BSSM dance teams, no uniforms or strict dress codes exist, but we do expect the dancers to dress modestly and we give them some general guidelines when it comes to dance clothes. These guidelines are for the dancers who minister on stage during the corporate worship times in BSSM.

BSSM worship dance dress code guidelines:

Dress like you are coming to worship Jesus with dance. Wear comfortable clothes that you can move easily in. Solid colors preferred to prints. You can wear ballet shoes or modern shoes, but barefoot is usually the best option on our stage.

Ladies: If wearing a skirt/dress, it needs to be at least knee length and you must wear leggings (not just tights) underneath. Leggings must cover knees. If skirt/dress flies all the way up when you spin, you must wear another skirt or slip underneath, or pin your skirt/dress to your leggings. If you choose to wear trousers instead of a skirt/dress, they need to have a wider leg and cover your knees (don't wear just leggings or shorts). Tops need to have high enough necklines that no cleavage shows when moving. Shirts need to be long enough, with no bellies or underwear showing. Wearing a leotard or a sports bra underneath is highly recommended. Don't just wear a leotard, but have another looser top over it. No bra straps showing and no see-through clothes.

Guys: Make sure your tops are long enough. No bellies or boxers showing. Pants should cover your knees. No shorts.

Some of these guidelines may seem ridiculously obvious, but it is helpful to have it all spelled out for the dancers to avoid misunderstandings. Of course these guidelines are not the only way for dance teams to dress, but for our teams, and in our cultural setting, these guidelines have been very helpful. The reason why we prefer solid colors to prints is we often use different colored silks when we dance, and it can look visually too busy with all kinds of patterns and combinations of many colors. The reason we ask the dancers to cover their knees is not so much for modesty's sake (even though this may be a good reason too), but more for the sake of protecting their knees as we often kneel down and move on the floor level as we dance.

Another aspect to consider is all the dancers have different shapes and sizes of bodies, and some clothes that may look good on one dancer, may not be too flattering or modest looking on another one. Common sense should be used when choosing what to wear. If you come from a professional dance world, our guidelines may sound very strict, and you may wonder why we don't let the dancers dance in just a leotard and tights. It is true that the beautiful lines dancers create with their bodies can sometimes be a little hidden under the layers of clothes, but we would rather lean toward being too careful than becoming a distraction to people. Even in our culture, dancing in worship is still quite a new concept for many people and we don't want to create any additional stumbling blocks.

In all of this, it's very important to always be motivated by love. I have needed to lovingly confront many of our dancers for not following our dress code. Most of the time it's not because they have a bad attitude, but because they have just forgotten. I actually bring some extra pieces of clothing with me whenever we dance in case someone has forgotten their dance clothes, but I do want the dancers to take responsibility for their own appearance. There have been times when I have needed to hold a dancer back from dancing on stage because they were not dressed appropriately. This is never out of punishment or control, but out of love and a desire to protect them.

6

Dancing on the Streets

Dance is such a powerful means of communication and shifting atmospheres. Once established, we should never keep our dance ministries only within the church walls. Through dance, we can embody movements and characteristics of the invisible world. Whether you have had years of dance experience or no dance experience, the profound revelation of who God is can manifest through you.

I have been overseeing the BSSM Dance Activation and City Service teams for four years now, and it has been amazing to see how God is moving in our city through dance. We have been dancing in many local neighborhoods, in several parks, in the downtown area, at the local mall, on a well-known bridge (Sundial Bridge), and even in people's houses. We always aim to be sensitive to the environment wherever we minister, and we have only ever received positive feedback the entire time we have been doing this. People become so happy when they see us dance, and we have been asked several times if this is an open dance class and if they could join us. Whether they know it or not, people feel drawn to us because of the atmosphere of Heaven we release through dance. Dancing creates a point of connection, and people who wouldn't otherwise talk to us are suddenly very approachable. The joy of the Lord takes people by surprise and makes their walls come down. We have been able to lead many people to Jesus and have seen people healed and set free in all kinds of places out on the streets. This is all very easily organized, and in most places you don't even need any permits when you dance, as long as you don't set up any big sound systems.

One time I took a team of about 15 dancers to a local park. We started by everyone doing freestyle dance and just having fun. As we were dancing, a man stopped in the middle of his biking trip and asked, *"Is it legal to have this much fun?!"* We laughed and invited him to come and join us. He actually danced with us for a little bit, and then a couple students prophesied over him and shared some words that God gave them for him. This man was deeply touched by God's love for him. He ended up receiving Jesus right there in the middle of the park! All of this happened simply because he was drawn to the atmosphere of joy that was being released through dance. Joy is one third of the Kingdom, and we should never underestimate the power of joy. *"For the kingdom of God is not a matter of eating and drinking, but of righteousness, peace and joy in the Holy Spirit"* (Romans 14:17).

Another time when we were dancing at the Sundial Bridge, a guy saw us dancing and asked one of our team members to swing dance with him, just for fun. While he was dancing, he realized his knee had been healed, and he recognized the manifest presence of God in that moment. I had never heard of anyone getting healed by swing dancing, but there are no limits to what God can do!

Block Parties

Our weekly dance outreach and City Service teams in BSSM have also been partnering with other teams that minister locally here in Redding. BSSM has some community teams that minister in different neighborhoods, build relational connections with the residents, and eventually start local home churches in those neighborhoods. The dance teams are sometimes invited to Block Parties, which the community teams throw for residents in various neighborhoods in Redding. There have already been many people saved through friendships that have developed between the locals and the community teams. One of the main purposes for having dancers at the block parties is to release freedom and joy in the atmosphere. The dancers can activate other people to dance as well. You can use any style of dance you like for an event like this. Many times the kids readily join us.

At block parties, we also offer to give prophetic words to people through dance. We don't necessarily call them prophetic words, but simply offer to do a dance for them personally. Afterward we explain what we felt while we were dancing. People are often amazed and wonder how we knew these things about them, or knew what was going on in their lives. We intentionally go after words of knowledge and ask God to give us information about the people we are ministering to. On one occasion, one of the dancers felt like God gave her the name Josh, and when we went out we met a guy whose name was Josh. He was so impacted that God called him by name, and for the first time he really believed God loved him.

You can create all kinds of parties or little gatherings in your own neighborhood, or join in when someone else is organizing an event. Whether it is a big or small event, it's easy to set up different stations. For example, you can allocate a specific spot where dancers can give encouraging words to people through dance. Once people see what you are doing, they usually become curious and start lining up to "receive a dance" for themselves. It's usually less threatening to people when they can come to you to receive a word, rather than you randomly stopping someone on the street to ask if you can dance for them. We have done dance ministry and multiple types of art booths at numerous types of events. There has always been a long line of people wanting to get danced over.

Flash Mob dances

Another form of dance we have been experimenting with is flash mob dances. Flash mob dances are rehearsed dances in which a large number of people perform at a predetermined location as a surprise to the rest of the people there. Usually they start with just a couple of dancers, and then gradually others join in. The vision behind our first flash mob dance was to bless the community, celebrate cultures, encourage creative expression, activate people in dance, and release unity, freedom, and joy. We did this flash mob dance in several places, including parks, market places, streets, and a community event. We even did it in a gas station in the middle of the night! More than 200 people learned the dance and did it at one of these places. We definitely met the goal of spreading joy, and some people were telling me it was the most fun event they were part of during the whole year. Dance can totally shift the atmosphere in the city. Once we had a group of people doing this same flash mob dance in downtown Duisburg, Germany in the middle of a cold and rainy day. We literally danced in the rain. The impact was very powerful, and we saw people's countenance change from depression to extreme joy.

Comments from students

It is wonderful to bless your own city through dance. As a dance pastor, one of my favorite things is to see the dancers step out of their comfort zones, take risks, and love people well. When I first started leading the dance teams that minister throughout Redding, I always went out with them so I could not only cover them in prayer, but also demonstrate how to minister to people on the streets and take risks. Later on, as our teams started growing, I started raising other leaders who could take different teams out. I believe the best way to lead is by example.

Here are some comments from the students from the BSSM Dance Activation / City Service:

"This activation has opened the door of freedom for me to be able to encounter God in a whole new way and to conquer the fear of doing things in public. I have experienced some of the most intimate times with God while dancing. There are times when words just aren't enough, and through dance I am able to express what my heart is saying. Dancing throughout areas in Redding has allowed me to cross my chicken line, step out, hear God's heart for this city, and release it in a way that is unexpected. There is a quote that says something like, "Go and preach the gospel and if necessary use words." That is what I feel like we are doing when we are dancing. We are displaying God's heart for this city. It is beautiful, powerful, beckons Heaven to invade earth, and people can't help but see that!" – Kelli

"One of the highlights for me was just overcoming my fear in dancing 'randomly' in places in public. The very first day we were taken down to Sundial Bridge and told to just dance, I

felt incredibly awkward and self-conscious, and didn't know what to do. But as I started dancing, I found a real freedom and joy in it. Another highlight happened downtown when I stopped dancing to talk to a woman who was passing by, and prayed for her. It is exciting to see how dancing draws people's attention and opens doors and they want to talk to you — people are often more open when they approach you rather than you approaching them." – Melinda

Some tips for outreach dance teams

• It is always best to be part of a team. Even if your whole team can't minister together, go out in groups of at least two or three as Jesus encouraged His disciples to do. Make sure you are looking out for one another.

• Acknowledge when someone steps out in faith, celebrate each breakthrough, and encourage one another to take it to another level, for example by expecting to have a word of knowledge for a person, offering to pray for healing, or inviting a person you have danced for to meet Jesus, who gave you the dance.

• Don't forget God celebrates risk, not just the outcome. When we trust Him and take steps of faith, He celebrates us.

• Have the whole dance team involved in sharing new ideas on how we can impact the city through dance.

• When dancing over a person on the street, don't use any "Christianese" (religious terms they may not understand). Always ask permission to do a dance for someone; don't just assume it is okay with them. The words and the dance you give should always be encouraging, positive, and uplifting. People should always feel like they have been "kissed by Jesus" when we minister to them, and at the very least leave, feeling loved and honored by us. A good guide is to check first if it was a dance you would enjoy receiving.

- Wear clothes that are comfortable for dancing. Check that you are dressed modestly and honor God and others by the way you dress. Even when we are not in a church building, we are always representing the Kingdom and we don't want to offend anyone or be distracting.

- Have fun! People are attracted to joy. If you enjoy what you do, it's likely others will enjoy it as well.

Intercession in public places

Some of our dance outreach teams go into strategic places around town to make declarations through dance. The main goal for these teams is not to connect with people, but to intercede for the city. When our teams go out to public places, and the main goal is not to minister to people, we still always want to be considerate to the people around us. We don't want to come across as weird or awkward on purpose. We are not ashamed to pray in public, but we want to honor people by the way we do our praying. Of course we are always called to take our lead from the Holy Spirit, and there may be times when our prayer meetings may seem strange for outsiders. The Holy Spirit can show up in unexpected ways, like on the day of Pentecost. Our goal, however, is not to try looking strange, but to honor God and honor our city and the people who live in it. There are many ways we can pray and make declarations through dance and movement. At the end of this chapter, two exercises are given to help prepare your dancers before going out.

Events to impact the city

We have also started exploring how we can run citywide creative arts events to bless our city. We would typically do these types of events a maximum of once a year because they take much more planning and preparation than our weekly outreaches. We want to give the city our best and run these events as professionally as possible, so we usually start preparing at the beginning of the school year. We create a production team and cast the vision. We book a venue, usually opting for something that's not a church facility in order to reach out to more people. We audition dancers, actors, musicians, visual artists, etc. This process takes a lot of work, but it's so worth it.

Last school year, our BSSM Kingdom Creativity track run an event called *i3 Awakened*, which was an interactive, creative arts event that was built around an original musical, and included drama, dance, and film. This event was held in the Redding Civic Center. Many people, who wouldn't necessarily attend a church service, encountered God's presence through this performance.

The dance classes at Bethel taught by INovia Dance have been performing dance pieces at fundraiser events for a homeless shelter in Redding. I have been teaching an improvisation class for INovia Dance, and last school year I created a "structured improvisation" piece for this event. Structured improvisation means it wasn't a choreographed dance, but it did have different sections when the dancers knew what type of movement they were creating. The dance also had a section when the dancers were taking turns in following each other's movement. Throughout the piece at random times, the dancers were also repeating a motif (a short phrase of movement, expressing the intention of the dance). My dancers danced to an instrumental song called "Overcoming Fear" and it was such a powerful declaration through movement, expressing how the love of God casts out all fear. Creating this kind of "structured improvisation" is a painless way of creating a performance piece. It doesn't take much time or planning, but it can be very powerful. It has been wonderful to get opportunities to impact the atmosphere in this city through dance during events like this.

Exercise 17. Declarations Through Dance

Arrangements:

Find some instrumental music. Have the dancers spread out all around the classroom.

First Phase – approximately one minute

Have the dancers close their eyes and ask God to give them one encouraging word for the city (e.g., hope, joy, salvation).

Second Phase – approximately five minutes

Turn on the music. Ask the dancers to start expressing the word they received for the city through dance. Encourage them to use different levels as they move.

Third Phase – approximately five minutes

Ask the dancers to take some time to come up with three still poses on three different levels to express the word they are declaring over the city. The first still pose should be on the floor level, for example kneeling down. *They can pretend there is an invisible ceiling that is at about their waist height, and the pose needs to be below it.* The second still pose should be half way up, for example one knee on the ground and arms reaching up. *They can pretend there is an invisible ceiling that is at about their shoulder height, and the still pose needs to be below it.* The third still pose is on the highest level, so they can do the pose as high as they can. They should only choose poses they are able to hold for at least 5 seconds. They can try using some similar shapes to the movements they used in the Second Phase.

Fourth Phase – approximately five minutes

Have the dancers pair up. Ask them to teach their three still poses to their partner. Ask them to also tell their partner what the word is that these poses express and symbolize.

Fifth Phase – approximately five minutes

By now all the dancers should have memorized two different words of declaration (one of their own and one from their partner) and six different still poses (three of their own and three from their partner). Turn on the instrumental music again. Have the dancers move from one still pose to another, using all six poses. They are free to do their own movements between the still poses and travel around the room. They don't need to do the poses in any particular order. Whenever they stop in one of the six poses, they should stay there for at least for 5 seconds. While they pause, they can say out loud the word that's connected with the pose. At this point, they don't need to dance close to their partner — they can move freely around the room.

Sixth Phase – approximately five minutes

Have the dancers find a new partner and teach their initial three still poses to them. Now all the dancers should have memorized three different words of declaration (one of their own and two from other dancers) and nine different still poses (three of their own and six from other dancers). The Fifth Phase may be repeated after having the dancers use all nine poses.

Debrief:

Give the dancers a chance to share how they felt about this exercise. Ask them to speak the words out loud that they received for the city.

My comments on this exercise:

This exercise is a great tool for teaching dancers to make declarations through movement. The Seventh Phase of this exercise would be to take a group of dancers to a strategic place in the city and have them repeat the Fifth Phase there. The movement in this exercise carries a powerful anointing to shift the atmosphere because it has been created very intentionally to bless the city with specific declarations. It is also visually beautiful to watch because of the mix of similar and different poses the dancers do, and because all the dancers use different levels in their poses.

Another reason this is so beautiful to watch is that many still moments occur in the midst of moving, which prevents the overall feeling from being too busy. When it's presented well, it can look like a choreographed dance piece. When we have done this exercise in different places, people have often stopped by to admire the beauty of the "presentation" and asked if we will be performing this piece again somewhere. This exercise also works without music, which is great if you don't have a sound system outside.

Exercise 18. Pictures

Arrangements:

Have the dancers form groups of 4-6 dancers, depending on how many dancers you have. Have half of the groups sit down and be ready to observe the groups that will be dancing first. Allocate a specific area in the dance studio for each group that is up for the first round. Find some instrumental music.

First Phase – approximately five minutes

Ask each group to come up with a specific word of declaration or blessing for the city — just one per group. Turn on the music. Tell the dancers to start dancing out their word in the allocated area for their group. They can use any style of dance they like. If one dancer stops and makes a still pose or shape expressing this declaration, the other dancers in the same group need to come and make a still pose or shape close to the dancer who stopped. Together they form a bigger still picture to make this declaration. They don't need to make similar looking poses to each other, but rather try to find how their shape would complement the bigger picture. They can use all levels for the picture. After everyone in the group has found their shape in the bigger picture, they can continue moving until the next dancer in the group makes another still pose and everyone in the group joins in.

Second Phase – approximately five minutes

Have the dancers who were observing swap places with the dancers who were dancing, and repeat the First Phase.

Third Phase – approximately five minutes

The Third Phase is almost the same as the First Phase, but this time ask the dancers to have some sort of physical contact with at least one of the dancers in their group as they do the still pictures. They can use their hands, feet, arms, legs, shoulders, elbows, backs, etc. to connect with another dancer. Everyone in the group should be connected to the big picture.

Fourth Phase – approximately five minutes

Have the dancers who were observing swap places with the dancers who were dancing, and repeat the Third Phase.

Debrief:

Ask the dancers to give feedback to the groups they were observing. Have them share if they saw any specific themes in the different pictures. Then ask them to share how this experience of creating pictures as a group felt for them while dancing. Was it easier or more challenging to create the pictures using physical contact? There are no wrong answers.

My comments on this exercise:

Like the previous exercise, this one also works well outdoors and for different outreach purposes. You don't even need music for doing this. You can give the dancers different themes to base their declarations on, depending on where you will be ministering. You can also create different atmospheres with this exercise. You can make it playful and fun, serious and deep, or anything in between.

Children and Dance

Children are so valuable in the Kingdom of God. Jesus Himself said: *"Let the little children come to Me, and do not hinder them, for the kingdom of heaven belongs to such as these"* (Matthew 19:14). The simplicity of their faith is inspiring and infectious. Children are like a secret weapon in the Kingdom. *"Through the praise of children and infants you have established a stronghold against your enemies, to silence the foe and the avenger"* (Psalm 8:2).

I believe children understand much more about the Kingdom of Heaven than we give them credit for. It's natural for children, and even babies, to start moving when they hear music. They are ready to respond, without any inhibition. In my experience, children are the ones who seem to be the most drawn to worship dance. I wonder if it's because they came from Heaven so recently they can still remember how the angels danced. Once when I was on a ministry trip in Germany, a young mother came up to me with her toddler. The mother told me her daughter could barely speak, but she had been pointing to me while I was dancing, and saying, "Angel, angel!" I don't know if she actually saw an angel dancing with me, but I'm sure there was something that reminded her of the reality of Heaven.

A couple of years ago, I was walking through the parking lot of a local grocery store, and a man holding a 3-year-old girl walked up to me. He asked if I was one of the dancers at Bethel. He said his little girl kept pointing at me, insisting she had seen me dance on TV. He figured it must have been while they were watching worship on iBethel TV. I find it hilarious that typically these little people are the ones who recognize me, but I consider it the highest honor. In all seriousness, I know there is something special about the way God is drawing little children into His presence through dance and worship.

Let the children dance

While I was on a ministry trip in Texas, I met a beautiful five-year-old girl. I asked if she would like to dance with me in worship. At first she looked very excited, but then her little heart sank as she whispered that she didn't think her father would approve of it. I was quite shocked to hear her response, but I encouraged her to go and ask her dad. After a moment, she ran back with her face glowing and said, *"My father said I can dance!"* Then she burst into a joyful dance and released great breakthrough and an atmosphere of freedom and joy in the room! In the same meeting, I also asked a young teenage girl to dance with me. She was quite hesitant at first, but then started expressing her love for the Lord in a beautiful dance. The girl's mom was moved to tears, and she told me her daughter had been told off for dancing at church when she was younger. Now God was bringing restoration and healing through dance. Immediately after that, an elderly woman pulled me aside and explained how she had always thought dance was just distracting at church, but this time God had touched her through dance in a deep way. Papa not only approves of His children dancing, He truly delights in it!

I understand there needs to be some order in the worship services, and I know the reasons why kids have often been told to sit still in the meetings. Nobody appreciates mad chaos. But it doesn't have to be chaotic. I have a big heart for releasing children in dance in ways that are actually helpful and fruitful for everyone. In the Bethel Healing Rooms, we have children who minister alongside the adults. In the next chapter, I will discuss the dance ministry in our Healing Rooms and share how we run the children's dance team there. We have seen God work in such powerful ways through the children. Their simplicity of faith both amazes and challenges me.

The other day, one of the kids on the Healing Rooms dance team said, *"Let's do the Peter thing!"* I asked her what she meant, and she explained she wanted to dance past the sick people so her shadow would fall on them and they would get healed. It would be just like Peter — as simple as that. We have seen many people receive both physical healing and inner healing by having the children's dance team minister to them, but just like all the other dancers, the children need pastoring. In many ways, their need for pastoral covering is even greater than the need of the adults. They need to know they are safe. Part of creating a safe place is having clear guidelines to let everyone to know when it's a good time and place to dance.

Healing, salvation, and encounters through dance

We have had wonderful opportunities to activate children in dance in the local public schools here in Redding. The BSSM Dance Activation and City Service teams have been part of an after school program for children since 2012. During the first year, we went to eight different schools to do dance ministry. These are not Christian schools, but because our church offers this program, we can freely bring our relationship with Jesus to the classes. It is awesome that we get to connect with and bless these children who might not otherwise even meet any believers. We teach the children about their identity in Christ through different dance exercises. We have seen many kids receive healing, both physically and for their hearts, through this dance ministry. At one of the schools, we asked the kids who had any sickness or pain in their body to gather in the middle of the room and we all danced over them, releasing God's healing presence. One boy immediately said his stomachache left, a girl said her sore throat was instantly healed, and another girl's foot injury was better. At another school, four kids with various aches and injuries were instantly healed! It is so much fun to demonstrate the goodness of God to children, and they have so much fun as they minister to one another through dance.

We have also seen kids fall in love with Jesus and receive Him as their Savior through dance ministry. Recently I had a dance ministry trip to Grand Junction, Colorado. I was invited to speak and dance at the opening meeting for Wake Up Sleeping Beauty, a ministry that reaches out to young girls. There were over 450 registered participants, and many of them were very young kids. I don't typically do altar calls for salvation on my dance ministry trips because most of the people attending my workshops are already believers, but I strongly felt to give these kids an opportunity to receive Jesus as their Savior. Just before the meeting started, I read an e-mail from my intern, telling me how several kids had just been saved as one of our BSSM dance teams ministered at an after school program. This felt like a confirmation that I should go for it as well. Such a sweet presence of the Holy Spirit came as I led multiple little kids to dedicate their lives to Jesus.

The following day, I was teaching a dance workshop hosted by the same ministry. I had prepared it for youth and young adults, so I was initially a little surprised when the majority of the participants were, once again, very young kids. I thought about quickly changing my plans, but I felt I should just go with all the exercises I had already prepared. This was a three-hour workshop. The first miracle to me was how all these little ones were so focused, and they participated without any problems throughout the workshop. Even more amazing was that they were having incredibly profound encounters with God. One little girl shared that while she was dancing, she felt Jesus stepping into her heart. She literally danced into salvation! Another young girl saw a vision of a waterfall while she was dancing, and she said Jesus wanted her to get baptized. A crowd of little children surrounded me, and they were describing what Jesus had shown them while they danced. Even the parents were amazed to hear what their kids were sharing.

Children don't have a "junior" Holy Spirit

I believe God wants to manifest His presence like we have never seen before through children. At Bethel, we often use the phrase, "Children don't have a junior Holy Spirit." It's true! It's the same Holy Spirit working through both children and adults.

I tasted this reality personally when I was a child myself (for more of my testimony, see the first chapter of *Encountering God Through Dance*). I have had the privilege of walking with Jesus and being filled with the Holy Spirit since I was a little girl. When I was 12 years old, I shared the gospel with my gymnastics friends, who were between the ages of 9 and 12. All seven of them gave their lives to Jesus, and it was an incredible testimony about the transforming power of the Holy Spirit in a tangible way. None of these kids came from Christian backgrounds. Two sisters were in this group, and their whole family was so impacted by how God moved in their lives, that they all ended up giving their lives to Jesus. First their mother came to the Lord, then their older sister, and later their father as well. Not only was he saved, he was also set free from alcoholism. After this, my parents and some other locals pioneered a children's ministry called King's Kids, which is part of YWAM's (Youth With a Mission) family work. We used a lot of creative arts in this ministry, especially dance. A big part of it was outreach and missions work, and we shared the gospel through dance in all kinds of places. As young kids, we experienced the presence and the power of the Holy Spirit, and saw people healed, saved, and delivered. These experiences and encounters left a lasting impact on all of us.

Children partner with the same God as the grown ups. Their encounters with God are as real as ours. Their ability to grasp Kingdom principles is often way greater than we presume. I have come to realize we don't always need to have simple, "child-friendly" exercises for training children to minister through dance. Some of these attempts can easily turn out to be too childish, even for the kids. I often use most of the same material with both kids and adults. I usually have a very wide age range of people attending my dance classes and workshops. As long as the children are motivated, they can stay focused and attentive for great lengths of time. Sometimes they can even be more focused when you have them practicing together with adults. Of course it's also great to have exercises that are specifically designed for children. Below are two examples of exercises to help children in their worship expression, and they can be used for adults as well. In my experience, most of the exercises in this manual work with both children and adults.

Exercise 19. Numbers

Arrangements:

Have the dancers spread out in the room so they can all see you. Tell them you will teach them ten still poses/ shapes, representing numbers from zero to nine.

First Phase – approximately five minutes

Demonstrate the ten different shapes below for the ten numbers. The shapes are not exactly like the numbers, but there is enough resemblance to help the children remember the poses.

Number 0. Crouch down with your hands on the floor and head down, forming as round of a shape as possible.

Number 1. Lie down on your stomach with your legs together and your arms stretched out straight, alongside your head. This is a flat number one, where you are completely prostrate, face down before the Lord. *We do it this way because we want to teach the kids to use different levels.*

Number 2. Go into a kneeling position, sitting on your knees. Keep your upper back slightly bent forward toward your knees, with your arms up and slightly curved, as an extension of your torso. Your face should be down, with your head between your arms. From the side, the shape of your body looks essentially like the number two.

Number 3. While still on your knees, sit up and lift your upper body, lift your arms and head up, doing a high release with your upper back bent backwards, and your arms as an extension of your torso. From the side, the shape of your body looks roughly like the number three.

Number 4. While still up on your knees, extend your right leg to the side, with your toes touching the ground. Lean your body to your left and place your left hand on the floor, holding the weight of your upper body, while reaching your right arm straight up in a vertical line toward Heaven. From the front, the shape of your body looks more or less like the number four.

Number 5. Stand to your feet, keeping your feet together in a parallel position, with your knees slightly bent. Keep your back slightly curved forward with your arms extended straight in a horizontal line as an extension of your torso. Your face is down, with your head between your arms. From the side, the shape of your body looks roughly like the number five.

Number 6. Stand on the tiptoes of your left foot, raising your left arm up and curving it toward your right side, bending your whole upper body toward your right. Simultaneously raise your right leg by lifting your right knee in a turn out position, the toes of your right foot touching your left leg, anywhere between your ankle and knee. You can fall out of this position by taking a step with your right foot across your left foot. From the front, the shape of your body looks essentially like the number six.

Number 7. Stand up straight with your feet together in a parallel position. Extend your arms straight in front of you horizontally with the palms of your hands facing up. From the side, the shape of your body looks nearly like the number seven.

Number 8. Stand with your feet turned out, bend your knees as much as you can without lifting your heals (plié). Lift your arms up, forming an oval shape over your head, with your fingertips nearly touching. From the front, the shape of your body looks more or less like the number eight.

Number 9. Stand up straight with your feet together in a parallel position. Extend your arms all the way up, doing a high release with your upper body with your upper back bent backwards, and your arms as an extension of your body. From the side, the shape of your body looks roughly like the number nine.

Second Phase – approximately five minutes

Have all the children repeat these number shapes a couple of times with you so they start remembering them. If you are working with younger kids, you can simplify these poses according to their skill level. You can play music while you do this.

Third Phase – approximately five minutes

Have the children do these shapes in any order they like. You can tell them to try doing their own phone numbers or any series of numbers they like.

Fourth Phase – approximately five minutes

Ask the kids to not only use these numbers, but to add their own traveling movement between the numbers. It is now up to them how much they want to use the numbers. Some of them may transition into doing just their own movements.

Fifth Phase – approximately ten minutes

Divide the kids into groups of three. Tell them to choose one topic to pray for. Give them time to come up with three different "pictures" that are made using any of the still poses for numbers from zero to nine. These three pictures will express their prayer. Here's an example of how they can pray for a sick relative by using three pictures:

Picture 1 – Have one dancer lie on the floor in the Number 1 pose, and the two other dancers on both sides in the Number 2 pose. The dancer in the middle represents the sick person, and the dancers on both sides represent people praying for the sick person.

Picture 2 – The dancer in the middle gets up into the Number 3 pose, and the other two come on both sides in the Number 5 pose. The dancer in the middle represents the sick person getting healed and getting up. The dancers on both sides represent God's covering over the person they are praying for.

Picture 3 – All the dancers get up into the Number 9 pose. This represents everyone thanking God for the healing.

This is just one example. They are free to express any prayer, using any of the numbers to create three different pictures. If the kids you are working with are younger, you can simplify this Phase by asking them to create just one or two pictures.

Sixth Phase – approximately one minute per group

Have all the groups of three present what they created. They can choose how they go from one picture to another when presenting the three pictures. Ask them to stay in one formation for at least 5 seconds. If you have a big group of dancers and not much time, you can have several groups presenting at the same time.

Debrief:

Ask each group to explain what their prayer was for.

My comments on this exercise:

Phases One through Five are great for teaching children to improvise movement. If you just tell children to move spontaneously, some of them may struggle with getting started. The numbers give them some movement vocabulary and help them use all the different levels in their movement. The numbers also become "safe places" where they can always go if they can't think of anything else to do. The still poses also help the kids understand the impact and the importance of pausing in the midst of movement. Even if the kids are too young to know their numbers, they can still mimic and memorize the still poses.

The Sixth Phase helps the kids make the connection between prayer and movement in a very concrete way. This exercise works well with people of any age who don't have much previous dance experience.

Exercise 20. Dancing Letters

Arrangements:

Have the dancers spread out evenly around the room. Find some instrumental music.

First Phase – approximately five minutes

Turn on the music. Tell the dancers to start writing the name of Jesus in the air, using different parts of their body to draw each letter. They can choose which body part they draw/paint with. For example, they could do J with their right hand, E with their left elbow, S with their right shoulder, U with their left knee, and S with the toes of their right foot. They can do this multiple times and try writing with different body parts.

Second Phase – approximately five minutes

Have the dancers ask God to give them one encouraging word. It could be, for instance, love, joy, hope, etc. It just needs to be something positive they can declare with their dance. Then have them draw this word using different body parts for each letter, just like in the First Phase.

Third Phase – approximately five minutes

Tell the dancers this time they will be painting letters on the floor instead of the air. The letters will be huge, and the dancers can find pathways with their whole body to "paint" the letters on the floor. They can imagine their whole body is covered with paint, and every time any part of their body touches the floor, it leaves a mark. They can use all the different levels as they move, but the goal is to find different floor patterns and do big traveling movements. Ask them to start again by "painting" the name of Jesus, one huge letter at a time.

Fourth Phase – approximately five minutes

Ask the dancers to repeat the Third Phase, but this time using the words from the Second Phase. Alternatively, you can ask them to paint the name of a person they want to pray for.

Debrief:

Ask the dancers to share the words they have been writing with their bodies.

My comments on this exercise:

This exercise helps the dancers use their whole body as they move and initiate movement with different body parts. The second half of the exercise helps them to find different floor patterns as they dance and use the space creatively. This exercise also helps the children to intentionally make a connection between declarations they make and their movement. If the kids you work with are too young to know how to spell, you can write some words on a whiteboard so they can try copying the shapes.

8

Healing Rooms Dancers

I have a big heart for seeing God's healing presence released through dance. One reason for this passion is that about 12 years ago, I went through quite an intense season of being very sick for nearly a year. I write more about my personal story and how God healed me in my first book, *Encountering God Through Dance*. The part I didn't feel released to share back then was that I had a very clear dream while I was sick. It's actually hard to say if it was a dream or a vision because I was in that in-between stage of being asleep and awake. In this dream, I saw a lady dressed in a white, long dress dancing toward me. She smiled and handed me a white dress to wear. It felt like some sort of an impartation, and I knew I was supposed to dance with this white dress. I don't quite know how, but somehow I knew this lady in the dream was Kathryn Kuhlman.

I was actually in a hospital when I had this encounter, and when I woke up or came out of the dream, my mom had just come to visit me. I asked her right away: *"Who is Kathryn*

Kuhlman?!" I may have heard her name sometime in the past, but I really had no clue who she was, or even if she was alive or not. My mom went to a library and borrowed a book for me about Kathryn Kuhlman. On the front cover there was a picture of her. I was stunned! There she was with that long white dress — just like in my dream. As I read the book, I came to discover how Kathryn was a healing evangelist who had gone to be with Jesus a bit over three years before I was born. I was really moved by reading the stories of people getting healed through Kathryn's ministry. I believe the reason why God showed me the dream about her was that He wanted to expand my heart for the sick and give me a passion for seeing people encounter God. I don't think I carry "Kathryn's mantle" or anything like that, but I believe I'm called to be part of raising up a generation of worshipers who operate in the healing anointing and release God's presence through all kinds of creative ways. I actually often wear white when I dance. And just to make it clear, I don't think I have to wear white in order to operate in my calling, but for me it's a practical reminder of the focus of my ministry.

One of my favorite places in the world is the Bethel Healing Rooms, which is a healing ministry we have here at Bethel Church every Saturday morning. It's like God's big playground where anything could happen! I started dancing with the Healing Rooms dance team the very first Saturday after moving to Redding. After a couple of months, I started co-leading the dance teams with my dear friend Christina. After Christina moved, I continued leading and building the teams. Now we have dance teams for both adults and children. Last year we also pioneered our first ever men's dance ministry in the Healing Rooms context. I have been part of the Bethel Healing Rooms dance ministry for over six years now. I have never missed a Saturday when I have been in town. I don't say this to brag about my commitment, but rather to demonstrate how much fun it is to partner with God in this setting and see people encounter the goodness of God personally.

Healing Rooms set up

I want to give you an overview of how we do dance ministry in our Healing Rooms setting. There are many ways to do it, but hopefully this gives you some ideas of how dance can be incorporated in different ministry contexts.

We used to have a "waiting room" for people who were waiting for personal prayer ministry. When people started getting healed while waiting there, we changed the name of this room to the Encounter Room. In the Encounter Room, we have a worship band playing live music. Our dance team ministers throughout the room (more on how we use the space is included later in this chapter). Artists paint prophetically on big canvases that are set up in the center of the room, while additional artists roam throughout the room, drawing smaller, personal prophetic pictures and portraits for our guests. We have intercessors, hospitality teams, pastoral teams, an inner healing team, and testimony writers. A Skype team ministers to people who can't physically come to the Healing Rooms. Several of the ministries within the Healing Rooms have four teams that rotate weeks, making the time commitment manageable for the volunteers (although many choose to come more often than required because it's such a great place to be).

Even with all these ministries happening at the same time, the Healing Rooms are not chaotic. Every Saturday we have an Encounter Room leader, who is directing where the entire room is going, both practically and spiritually. The leader helps in communicating to our guests when it's their turn to receive personal ministry and shares testimonies throughout the morning. The leader also communicates to the whole room when specific themes arise that the intercessors, and/ or the other ministry teams, feel God is doing in the room. As the dance team leader, I communicate with the Encounter Room leader throughout the morning.

The main purpose of the Encounter Room is to offer a place where people can just receive and encounter God. We don't want to only know that God is our Healer, we want to *encounter* Him as our Healer. We don't want to only know that God is our joy and freedom, we want to encounter Him and the fullness of His joy and freedom. Our worship teams (musicians, dancers, and artists) are all hosting God's presence and personally encountering God. We don't only sing, dance, and paint about Him, we do it all *with* Him, experiencing His presence with us. I think this is the main reason why we all love ministering in the Bethel Healing Rooms so much!

We use our main Sanctuary as the Encounter Room, and from here people are called out in groups to go into another room where they receive personal ministry from our ministry teams. We also offer classes both before and after people receive ministry. The class beforehand is called "Encounter the Healer" and the class afterward is called "Walking in God's Best for Your Health."

All the teams arrive at 8am to pray, set everything up, and to be soaked in God's presence until we are all fully filled and ready to pour out. Our dance team stretches and warms up during this first hour as well. The musicians and some of the set-up crew actually arrive even earlier in the morning to prepare. Our guests start coming to the Encounter Room at 9am and we usually minister to them until around noon. It is quite a long time for the dancers to minister, so we take breaks as needed. At the very end, we all circle up to share testimonies of what God has done throughout the whole morning. It's extremely important for us to give God the glory and celebrate what He has done. We have seen all kinds of crazy miracles: blind eyes open, deaf ears hear, tumors disappear, and hearts are healed in God's presence (to name a few). Hundreds of visitors receive ministry on any given Saturday.

Partnering with God and one another

We all partner with God and with one another. As dancers, we are there to come alongside the rest of the worship team and serve them. However, as the relationship between the different teams grows stronger, it is beautiful to see how we take turns in leading one another. Many times the worship leaders and musicians have told us afterward that they were following the dancers and taking their cues from us. We, likewise, have often taken the lead from the artists and started expressing the same themes through dance that they have been painting on their canvases. Many times we also "unintentionally" dance with the same colors of silks that the artists are painting with. Every week we go on this grand adventure with God and one another.

As dancers, our main focus is to shift the atmosphere in the room. In practical terms this happens through our uninhibited, unrestrained worship — our whole spirit, soul, and body praising God. When most of our guests come in, they are often very focused on their sickness and pain. We want them to focus on God instead. We intentionally draw them into God's presence through movement and dance. The setting in the Encounter Room gives us a lot of freedom. It's all very organic, without a set formula. We are all constantly listening to what the Holy Spirit is doing and looking for ways to partner with Him.

We have had different room configurations throughout the years. However the room is set up, a space is always dedicated for the dancers to minister in, both on stage and around the room. At present, the chairs our guests sit in are placed in big, concentric circles, with additional rows of chairs around the parameter of the room. This set up gives the dancers space between the rows and circles of chairs, and along the sides, back, and front of the room, to minister to our guests who sit there. We can also get close to the artists who paint in the middle of the room, which makes it easier for us to partner with them in a practical way and connect with what they are doing. We also have a great deal of room on stage — more than in other ministry settings at Bethel. The worship band is set up so far back that our dance team has ample space, both in front of the band and on the side sections of the stage. This makes it easy for the dancers and the musicians to partner together because we can see each other so well. It also gives us opportunities to have bigger groups of dancers minister on stage. There have been times when I have had about 20 dancers dancing on stage at the same time. This may sound like it could create chaos, but it's amazing to see how beautifully it all flows as we follow God's lead. The more the dancers spend time ministering together, the easier it gets for them to tune into what God is doing and, at the same time, to partner with one another. There is so much harmony that it often feels like our dances have been choreographed in Heaven. Once I sent 18 dancers on stage at the same time, and people literally thought we had choreographed "the piece" because everyone was so in sync.

We often dance around the whole room, and at times we activate the entire room to dance with us. Sometimes we dance together as one big team, and other times we split into smaller teams. If we feel like God is highlighting a certain person to us, we ask them if they would like the dance team to minister to them personally. Sometimes the ministry team members will ask if the dancers can dance over a specific person they have been ministering to. Whenever we dance over people and minister to them personally, I always make sure no one is doing it alone. We have this same guideline for the Healing Rooms prayer ministry teams — we never minister alone. It is always safer and more effective to minister as a team.

We have so many fun and incredible testimonies of God touching and healing people through dance ministry. We have come to discover how much God loves partnering with us. He is the Creator and He can do creative miracles by Himself, but He loves it when His children partner with Him in creative ways to release His Kingdom.

Healing Rooms testimonies

Some time ago, our Healing Rooms dance team ministered to a lady who hadn't been able to dance for eight years. She had undergone surgery on her feet and had a lot of pain in one of her ankles and particularly in one of her big toes. She had a metal screw inside her big toe, which prevented her from standing on her toes. As we released God's presence and danced over her, she was moved to tears — happy tears. At first some of the pain left, then all the pain left, and after all these years of not being able to stand on her toes, she could finally do it again! She actually started dancing and jumping all around the stage! Afterward she told us she couldn't find or feel the screw anymore. She was not only physically healed, God had also restored her hope and dream to start leading a dance ministry.

We also like experimenting with fun and new things with our dance team. On a Saturday just before Valentine's Day, one of the dancers brought some flowers to the Healing Rooms. We started dancing with the flowers and then handed them out to some individuals who we felt God was highlighting to us. Many people were in tears as they received God's love in a concrete way. The same morning, one of the prayer servants had a word of knowledge about God healing people who didn't have the sense of smell. A man who couldn't smell anything received one of the flowers, and his sense of smell was instantly restored as he smelled the flower!

One Saturday morning we ministered to a woman who told us she used to love dancing when she was a child. Later on in her life she had been sexually abused, and hadn't been able to dance since then. Every time she tried to dance she started having so much physical pain all over her body that she just couldn't move. We discerned this was more of a spiritual than a physical issue, but God is bigger than anything causing pain. She asked if we could release God's presence over her by dancing. As we were dancing, her countenance completely changed, and she started expressing her love for God with the most graceful movements. Her whole appearance looked different, and she cried out, *"I have no more pain!"* God set her free in such a beautiful way.

Recently, as our dance team was dancing around the Encounter Room, we felt drawn to a lady who was sitting in a wheelchair. Her face was completely pale, and we found out she had stage four breast cancer. As we started dancing around her, we saw her countenance change, and color started returning to her face. All of a sudden she started moving her arms in worship, and then she literally got up from her wheelchair and started twirling and dancing with us! Afterward she shared that she hadn't been able to get up from her wheelchair for a week, and now she felt strength coming back to her body. She will of course need to see a doctor to get tested, but she looked like a different person after the ministry time!

Children in the Healing Rooms

As I mentioned before, we also have children ministering in the Bethel Healing Rooms. Our goal is not to have a separate children's ministry, but rather to include them in our regular dance teams as much as possible. We often pair the children up with one or two of the older dancers. We also often dance together as a whole team. At times the children follow us, and at times we give them opportunities to lead us. The more the dancers minister together, the easier it becomes to follow one another and to flow spontaneously as a team. I do direct some of the things we do by verbally giving some instructions, but I prefer the times when the whole team is so tuned in with each other and with the Holy Spirit that I don't need to tell anyone what to do. They all spontaneously take turns in leading and following, partnering with God and with one another.

On our official team, we welcome children between the ages of 6 and 12. Our ministry times are quite long, so children who are younger than six can find it difficult to stay focused for the whole morning, even when we have official break times for them. However, we do make exceptions and at times let younger kids join in, as long as their parents are nearby so they can pick up the kids if they become too tired. One year we had a girl who was only five years old, but she was more focused than most of the older kids. She was a huge blessing for the whole team, and released God's presence in such a powerful way, that we learned sometimes age doesn't matter. We currently have the children with us every other Saturday. They are split into two ministry teams that rotate weeks, which means every child on the team gets to dance with us about once a month.

We also have children who minister in the Healing Rooms through prophetic art and by praying for people with their "big brother" or "big sister." These "siblings" are adults on our ministry team who have a heart for children. When a child is interested in ministering in the Bethel Healing Rooms, their parents fill out an application form. If the child specifically wants to dance in the Healing Rooms, the children's ministry leader contacts me, and I schedule a time when the child can come and have a "try out" with our team. This is not a formal audition. We invite the child to come dance with us once or twice in the Healing Rooms as a "try out." This allows the child to experience what it's like to dance and be part of the team, and to express if she/he would like to continue as a team member. The "try out" time also gives me, as the leader, a chance to see if it feels like the new dancer is a good fit for our team, and allows the rest of the team to give me input. I don't necessarily require the children to have any previous dance training, but in order to minister with us, the child needs some basic body awareness and spatial awareness. Dance training is of course very helpful, but if a child has a general understanding of movement and some coordination skills, they can always learn more technical skills along the way. Even more importantly, we look for children who have a heart after God.

Adult dance teams in the Healing Rooms

Our application process for adults is actually very similar to the children's process. The only difference is the adults go through Bethel's ministry team training before they can apply for the dance team. We also have a written application for the adults so we can find out more about their background in dance and their heart for the healing ministry. Just like with the children, we ask the adults to "try out" at least once or twice before we officially invite them to be members of our team.

This past year, we started accepting men on our dance teams for the first time. We hadn't had many of them wanting to do dance ministry in previous years, and consequently we only had women. But they just started flooding in this year, so it felt like perfect timing to launch a men's dance team. Initially we started having the men join us only once a month, but they were such a great addition to our ministry that we started inviting them to join us every other week. For practical reasons, and to keep the numbers for our teams balanced, we usually rotate the children's and men's teams. So we have the kids with us every other week, and the men join us for the weeks the children aren't there. Having the men with us feels like a missing piece of the puzzle has found its spot at last.

Men release something very powerful with their dance — a distinctive strength and grace is released that can only be given to us through our brothers. I'm not saying the men on the team are more important than the ladies; I'm saying both men and women have their own unique flavor that's very much needed. Clearly not all the men dance in the same way or have the same style, just like not every woman dances the same way. I never tell the men to try to dance like a man, in the same way I would never tell the ladies to try to dance like a woman. I believe I understand the reason why some people tell the men on their dance teams to "dance like a man" — they probably have not seen many examples of men dancing (especially at church), and they are trying to make sure the men know they don't need to copy the ladies. However, I would rather encourage the entire team to just relax, be themselves, and release God's presence in the way that's most natural for them. Some men's movement styles are more graceful, and some are more energetic or robust. There is no right or wrong way of moving. Regardless of their movement style, the men release something very unique through their dance, and it has been a real honor to have them join our team.

Skype Ministry

Another way we do ministry in the Bethel Healing Rooms is through Skype calls. I'm sharing about this method to help you think outside the box, and to give you some ideas for doing dance ministry in non-traditional ways. As I mentioned before, people who can't make it to the Healing Rooms in person can call us via Skype and receive ministry through the Internet. As a dance team, we sometimes dance in front of the computers, thus ministering to people in other cities and countries.

One Saturday I felt like we should go and dance near the computers being used for the Skype ministry. I felt drawn to a specific computer and asked the ministry team member who was on that computer if we could partner with him in ministering to the woman who was on Skype with him. He was happy to let us join in, and we learned the lady who was calling at that moment was a German missionary in Finland — my home country! Someone had just recently given her my book *Encountering God Through Dance*. She was delighted to let us minister to her through dance. She had leukemia, and one of the healing testimonies I share in that book is about a little girl who was healed from leukemia through dance. The little girl was so sick that she couldn't come to the Healing Rooms, but her parents came and brought a picture of her to me, and they asked me if I could lift her up to Jesus as I was dancing. The next time I saw this little girl's parents, they told me she was out of the hospital and doing really well! It was a heavenly setup that the woman on Skype had just read this testimony. As our dance team danced over her through Skype, she powerfully encountered God's presence. I haven't been able to follow up on how she is doing now, but it was definitely a divine appointment. How amazing is it to live in the days when we can use technology to minister through dance to people all around the world!

Building community and training with each other

Our dance teams within the Bethel Healing Rooms have grown quite rapidly in numbers during the past couple of years. We have many BSSM students who do the Healing Rooms dance team as their City Service, which is their weekly outreach. We have two different student rotations that minister every second week, and we also have dancers who are not in BSSM. The minimum level of commitment for the non-student dancers is to dance once a month, with one of the four teams we have on rotation. Most dancers want to come at least twice a month. Since we have so many different teams, we also meet outside of the Healing Rooms to connect and build community. We typically meet once or twice a month. Some of these meetings are just fun, hang-out times, but we also intentionally minister to one another and dance together.

For our meetings and connection times, the emphasis changes during different seasons. At the beginning of the school year, when a whole new group of dancers from BSSM joins us, we spend more time dancing together outside of the Healing Rooms than the rest of the year. This gives us a chance to connect as a team before we start ministering to others together. When we added the men's teams, we did a class for just men to help them get connected. Right now we have several new kids on our children's team, and they are in need of more intentional mentoring and practical teaching in dance. In order to address this need, we are offering additional dance classes for them.

We don't typically use our team times for learning dance technique, but we do encourage our dancers to take technique classes and develop their technical skills. We use many of the exercises in this manual during our team times. At the end of this chapter, there are examples of the type of exercises that will help dancers grow in their creative expression. We have also started creating some short phrases of choreographed movement in our classes. Even though most of our dance is spontaneous in the Healing Rooms, it has been fun to explore adding some choreographed phrases of movement in the midst of the improvised movements. We have intentionally created these movement phrases together as a group, partnering with God. When everyone has been part of the process of creating the movements, everyone feels ownership and connection to them.

Exercise 21. The River –
Initiating Movement with Different Body Parts

"The man brought me back to the entrance to the temple, and I saw water coming out from under the threshold of the temple toward the east (for the temple faced east). The water was coming down from under the south side of the temple, south of the altar. He then brought me out through the north gate and led me around the outside to the outer gate facing east, and the water was trickling from the south side. As the man went eastward with a measuring line in his hand, he measured off a thousand cubits and then led me through water that was ankle-deep. He measured off another thousand cubits and led me through water that was knee-deep. He measured off another thousand and led me through water that was up to the waist. He measured off another thousand, but now it was a river that I could not cross, because the water had risen and was deep enough to swim in — a river that no one could cross... where the river flows everything will live" (Ezekiel 47:1-5, 9b).

This exercise is based on the passage of Scripture above, explaining the vision God showed Ezekiel about the River of Life. *You can read it out loud to the dancers before you get started.*

Arrangements:

Have the dancers spread out all around the studio. Find some instrumental music. If you have a song about the River of God, it would work really well for this exercise.

First Phase – approximately three minutes

Tell the dancers they are stepping into the River of Life. At first their toes get wet. Ask them to start initiating movement with their toes. They can do this either one foot at a time or both feet together. It's up to them how much they move other parts of their body, but every movement should start from their toes, and then it can spread to the rest of their body.

Second Phase – approximately three minutes

Tell the dancers the water level is coming up to their knees. Ask them to start initiating movement with their knees. They can do it one knee at a time or both knees together. Again, it's up to them how much they move other parts of their body, but every movement should start from their knees, and then spread to the rest of their body.

Third Phase – approximately three minutes

Tell the dancers the water level is coming up to their waist. Ask them to start initiating movement first with their hips, then with their ribcage, and the movement spreads to the rest of their body like in the previous Phases. Please note: *Using your hips or your ribcage to initiate movement can be done in a pure way. In other words, it doesn't need to be sensual or sexual at all. It's great for dancers to practice using their whole body as they dance.*

Fourth Phase – approximately three minutes

Tell the dancers the water level is getting even deeper. Ask them to start initiating movement first with their shoulders, then with their elbows, then with their hands, and lastly with their head.

Fifth Phase – approximately three minutes

Tell the dancers they are fully submerged and can swim and dive in the river. They can spontaneously choose any body part to initiate these movements, but ask them to be aware of which body part is initiating their movement.

Debrief:

Ask the dancers what this experience was like for them.

My comments on this exercise:

This exercise is great for teaching dancers to initiate movement with different body parts. Often when you come to the Fifth Phase, the dancers feel a whole new level of freedom and creativity in their movement expression.

Exercise 22. Psalm 23 – Motif exercise

Arrangements:

Have the dancers spread out around the studio and lie on the floor. Find some instrumental music.

First Phase – approximately three minutes

Ask the dancers to just rest and breath, and read Psalm 23 out loud to them.

"The Lord is my shepherd, I lack nothing. He makes me lie down in green pastures, He leads me beside quiet waters, He refreshes my soul. He guides me along the right paths for His name's sake. Even though I walk through the darkest valley, I will fear no evil, for You are with me; Your rod and Your staff, they comfort me. You prepare a table before me in the presence of my enemies. You anoint my head with oil; my cup overflows. Surely Your goodness and love will follow me all the days of my life, and I will dwell in the house of the Lord forever."

Second Phase – approximately three minutes

Read Psalm 23 again, this time asking the dancers to start moving to the words.

Third Phase – approximately three minutes

Ask the dancers if there was a word or phrase in the Psalm that stood out to them. Ask each dancer to create a gesture or a simple movement phrase for the part of the Psalm that stood out to them. Emphasize keeping it very short and simple.

Fourth Phase – approximately three minutes

Have the dancers divide into groups of four to six, depending on how many dancers you have. Within these groups, have each dancer teach the others their gesture or the simple movement phrase they have created.

Fifth Phase – approximately three minutes per group

Ask each group to choose two of the gestures or short movement phrases from their group to be used as a motif — a recurring theme for this next part of the exercise. Have one group at a time do an improvisation, in which they will use these two motifs. They can dance any style, and they are free to do any of their own movements inspired by the Psalm, but ask them to connect as a team and be aware of one another. Most importantly, ask them to do these motifs of their choice several times in different places throughout the dance. Turn on the track of instrumental music you have chosen. If you have many groups and not much time, you can have more than one group go at a time. Just have them share the space. The dancers who are not dancing will be observing, sitting by the walls of the studio.

Debrief:

> Ask the dancers who were observing to share about what they saw. What stood out for them? How did the dance make them feel?

My comments on this exercise:

> I find this exercise especially powerful because the Word of God inspires the movements. You could use any Scripture for doing this exercise. It also helps the dancers to understand how powerful it is to do simple gestures and movement phrases. As you will probably discover during the debrief time, the gestures that are repeated frequently really stand out from the other movements. This is a great tool for choreographing dance pieces. Dancers can also learn to pick up gestures from one another spontaneously, and use them as motifs as they dance and improvise together.
>
> If you have more time for doing this exercise, you can ask the dancers to choose two other motifs that the dancers in their group had created and repeat the Fifth Phase using them.

9

A Heart of a Pastor

My heart leaps for joy when I see my dancers growing and maturing in the Lord, and releasing the true heartbeat of Heaven. I can relate to what John said: *"I have no greater joy than to hear that my children are walking in the truth"* (3 John 1:4). As a dance pastor, there is no greater joy than to hear that my dancers are worshiping and dancing in the Spirit and in truth! One of my dancers from BSSM gave this feedback for the Bethel Healing Rooms dance ministry:

"It was one of my highlights this year. I've had a real struggle in the past with stepping out and dancing with the Holy Spirit, but with the dance team it was so natural and easy. I've never been in a dance environment like this, where there's no performance and competition about being the best. Now I want to bring a lot of this back home."

Comments like this make it all worth it for me. I absolutely love it when my students release the heartbeat of Heaven corporately in worship. What makes me even happier is when I can see they are personally growing in the fruit of the Spirit — when I see their love for one another and for the Lord is genuine and real. In times when their joy abounds even in the midst of the currents of life crashing over them, and they abide in peace regardless of their circumstances. When they are patient while facing mountains that haven't moved yet, respond with kindness even when they are exhausted, leak the goodness of God in dark places, and serve with faithfulness and heartfelt commitment. When they give a gentle answer even if wrongly accused, and exercise self-control when facing various kinds of temptations.

"But the fruit of the Spirit is love, joy, peace, forbearance, kindness, goodness, faithfulness, gentleness and self-control. Against such things there is no law" (Galatians 5:22-23).

If I want to see my dancers grow in the fruit of the Spirit, the best thing I can do is to cultivate the presence of God in my own life. The best way to learn something is by following the example of others. My actions speak louder than my words. I'm not striving to be perfect, but my goal is to live so close to the only One who is perfect that His character traits start rubbing off on me. When I stay close to Him, the fruit of the Spirit should follow as the natural overflow from my life. When you lean on the Holy Spirit, striving ceases.

As a dance pastor, I believe the most important thing is that you have a heart after God, and the second most important thing is that you have a heart for people. In order to lead and pastor dancers, you don't need to be a highly skilled, technically advanced dancer. Having some technique training and understanding of movement is always helpful, but as a pastor, your heart is way more important than your technical ability. I have been leading and pastoring many dancers who are on a much higher level in dance technique than I am, and it doesn't disqualify or threaten me at all. Quite the opposite — I'm thrilled that God trusts me with trained dancers, and they are often the ones whose hearts need a great measure of pastoral support.

Learning to communicate

Communicating well, and teaching your dancers to communicate well, is one of the keys in pastoring dancers. I would say it's actually one of the most important skills, not only in pastoring, but also in life. Dancers are communicators. That's what they do through their dance. Sometimes dancers just haven't developed their verbal communication skills, especially when it comes to communicating their feelings. It may be much more natural for them to communicate their hearts through movement, and that may even be one of the reasons why they started dancing to begin with. Dancers can be amazing at communicating through movement, but not always as comfortable expressing themselves through words. One of my goals is to help them start articulating what they feel and see as they dance. As a pastor, I always want to cover and protect the hearts of my dancers, but I also want to challenge them to move forward and take risks so they can grow. This is one of the reasons why every exercise I have written in this book has a debrief section at the end.

Part of communicating well as a pastor is getting all the practical information to the dancers on time. I'm running so many different dance teams in BSSM that I jokingly say I have turned into a queen of communication. I write a ridiculous amount of e-mails every day — reminders to the dancers about the class times and locations, rosters for who is dancing at which meeting, and replies to countless e-mails about dance related things in our community. I use multiple ways of communicating: e-mail, Facebook, text messaging, phone calls, and in person. I don't think we can ever communicate too much. I'm a firm believer in clear communication, and I think it's one of the foundational building blocks for any ministry. No matter how anointed you are, you can't pastor people well if you don't learn to communicate effectively.

As a pastor, you also need brave communication skills. We need to learn to confront people in love when needed. We expect the dancers who are actively serving on our ministry teams to cultivate lifestyles that glorify God. The goal is never to control anyone, but rather, as fathers and mothers, to help people take ownership of their lives and grow in maturity, wholeness, and Christlikeness. In order to speak into people's lives, we need to have a certain level of "relational capital" with them. They need to know we have their ultimate best in our minds and we genuinely love them. Good communication is one of the building blocks for "relational capital," but even more importantly, people need to know we believe in them. Encouragement and believing in people are such powerful tools for lasting transformation. The Apostle Paul says beautifully:

"For you know that we dealt with each of you as a father deals with his own children, encouraging, comforting and urging you to live lives worthy of God, who calls you into His kingdom and glory" (1 Thessalonians 2:11-12).

We don't expect people to make messes, but if it happens, we need to help them clean up their messes. A great resource that has excellent teaching on communication is Danny Silk's book *Keep Your Love On.* I highly recommend it to everyone. Danny's book also has great teaching on having healthy boundaries. As a dance pastor, having good boundaries is another vital element. You need to learn to take care of yourself so you can take care of others as well. Sometimes this means saying no when people ask you to do things, which helps you have energy to say yes when God asks you to do something.

Discerning seasons and embracing the new

As a dance pastor, I always want to be tuning into what God is doing in the current season. When Jesus walked on the earth, He expressed how intently He focused on what the Father was doing:

"Jesus gave them this answer: 'Very truly I tell you, the Son can do nothing by Himself; He can do only what He sees His Father doing, because whatever the Father does the Son also does" (John 5:19).

Jesus was energized and nourished by doing the will of the Father:

"My food," said Jesus, *"is to do the will of Him who sent Me and to finish His work"* (John 4:34).

It's crucial for us to continually tune into what the Father is doing. This can save us from unnecessary stress, from spreading ourselves too thin, and even from getting burnt out. We don't need to be the answer for all the problems in the world; we simply get to be nourished by the things the Father is asking us to do.

In different seasons, our focus needs to change. Human nature is typically not very fond of change, and that's why transition times can feel difficult for many of us. However, when we learn to partner with God in what He is doing in different seasons, it often makes transitions and stepping into new things not just bearable, but fun!

The nature and the character of God don't change, and His Word doesn't change, but the way He does things can change. The way He asks us to do things can change as well. The book of Exodus contains the story of Moses leading the Israelites through the desert into the Promised Land. God asked Moses to give the Israelites water by striking the rock at Horeb. As Moses obeyed the Lord, water gushed out of it for people to drink (Exodus 17). Later, the people were thirsty again. This time, God told Moses to speak to the rock to bring water out of it (Numbers 20). Moses, however, decided to follow the previous plan rather than listen to God, and he struck the rock again. God, in His mercy, still gave water to the people, but because Moses didn't do it God's current way, he was denied access to the Promised Land. I'm not a theologian, and I'm not trying to be one, but I'm sure there are multiple ways of looking at this scripture. Some people say Moses couldn't enter the Promised Land because he represented the law. Others say it was because the rock represented Christ, who was to be struck only once. In any case, this is a very sobering word about the importance of moving with the current heartbeat of Heaven. We enter into God's promises by being current in our relationship with Him, not necessarily through old traditions. As seasons change, often God's emphasis will as well. We shouldn't yell what God is whispering, and we shouldn't whisper what He is shouting.

In order to lead dancers well, a dance pastor needs to learn to embrace the new things God is doing. We need to learn to hold our ways of doing things lightly and be willing to change. I want to re-emphasize that this manual is not intended to present the only way of doing dance ministry. The core values that you build on should always be steady, but their practical applications in various places and seasons may look different. When it comes to the practical exercises, God may very well show you something new that's not mentioned in this manual. We are all on a journey with God, and He is constantly doing new things. *"Do not dwell on the past. See, I am doing a new thing! Now it springs up"* (Isaiah 43:18b, 19a). He is the Creator and loves co-creating with us.

Using the right keys

God spoke to me about the principle of entering into His promises through quite a funny incident last year. I came home after a long day and stood outside my apartment. I was holding my car remote, pointing it several times toward my house door, and wondering why the door wasn't opening. It was one of those days. Once I finally figured out why the door wasn't opening, I heard God say, *"The key you are holding is not a fake key, it's just that it's meant for another door."* Then I heard Him again, this time saying, *"Testimonies are a key. They are an important key that you need. But the key you need in this season is the promises for the future."* This phrase ended up literally giving me a solution for a very important practical dilemma I was facing at the time. I was in the process of applying for an extension for my visa, and in the paperwork I had given my testimony of how I had been able to live in the USA as a volunteer for the past two years. The government officials were initially not convinced I would be financially stable enough to stay here if I continued as a full-time volunteer. It wasn't until I sent them *the promises* — in the form of letters from different churches who had invited me to come and minister during the upcoming season and promised to sow into my ministry financially — that they approved the petition.

Consequently, this word about promises being the key was literally a key to entering my promised land. Even though this was a specific word for a specific situation, I also believe it is a corporate word God is speaking in this season for the Bride of Christ as a whole. Testimonies are powerful, and we should never forget what God has done in the past, but I believe it's time for us to lift up our eyes, look into His promises, and let them open the doors of our destinies. It's time to believe and dream again. Promises are always relational — they depend on the faithfulness of the heart of the one who made the promise. We can have our hearts in a place of perfect peace and abundant hope *"for He who promised is faithful"* (Hebrews 10:23b).

Exercise 23. Healing for Hearts

As a pastor, my heart is to see the dancers made whole and healed from any hurts of the past, having their minds renewed in God's presence. This exercise is designed to help the dancers receive healing for their hearts and position them to receive all that God has for them.

Arrangements:

> Have the dancers stand in a line along the back wall of the dance studio, about two arms' length away from one another. If it's too crowded, you can make a staggered line, in which every other dancer takes two steps forward, so everyone has enough space around them. Or you can split the dancers into a couple of groups and repeat the exercise twice so everyone has a chance to participate. If you do the latter option, the dancers who are waiting can be

the intercessory team for the others. Find three different tracks of instrumental music. Tell the dancers they will be dancing in three spots across the room. They will be moving straight forward, making a pathway across the room, like a timeline that includes places for three memories. The first dance spot is close to the back wall, the second one is near the middle of the room, and the third one is close to the front wall of the room.

First Phase – duration approximately five minutes

Turn on the first track of instrumental music. Have the dancers ask the Holy Spirit to remind them of some breakthrough they have already received in their lives — a memory they are thankful for. This could be, for example, when they first got saved. Once their hearts are connected to that memory, ask them to start expressing their thankfulness to God through dance.

Second Phase – duration approximately five minutes

Turn on the second track of instrumental music. Ask the dancers to take a few steps forward, and come into a new spot in the center of the room. Have them ask the Holy Spirit to show them if any place in their heart has pain and needs healing. For example, He may reveal a memory of failure or a disappointment in some area of their lives. Tell them they don't need to try digging up things God has already healed, but they can ask the Holy Spirit to highlight if anything needs to be dealt with at this time. Once their hearts are connected to that memory, they can start releasing it to God through dance. As they are dancing, they can also ask God to show them where He was in that memory. Ask them to invite the Holy Spirit into that memory.

Third Phase – duration approximately five minutes

Turn on the third track of instrumental music. Ask the dancers to take a few steps forward, and come into a new spot toward the front of the room. Have the dancers ask the Holy Spirit to remind them of one specific promise they have received from God. This could be a Scripture or any personal promise God has given them in the past. You can also give them the option of asking God for a new promise. Tell the dancers this is a prophetic act of them stepping into their promised land and activating their faith to take hold of the promises God has given them.

Debrief:

Ask the dancers to write down anything specific God spoke to them during this exercise. You can also ask if any dancers feel like sharing part of their encounter/experience with the group.

My comments on this exercise:

I have personally seen many dancers receive deep healing for their hearts through this exercise. It's extremely important that the part dealing with painful memories happens between "thankfulness" and "the promises." This helps the dancers approach God from the place of thankfulness and leaves them in a place of grateful expectancy.

Exercise 24. Impartation

God has given all of us a different type of grace and anointing in our lives. Freely we have received, and freely we can give. We can't impart our personal history with God — people need to walk that journey on their own — but we all have something to bless others with.

I love being able to bless my dancers and impart to them what I have. Here is one simple example of how this can be expressed.

Arrangements:

> Have all the dancers lay on their backs on the floor, evenly spread out all around the room. Turn on some soft instrumental music or worship music. Have a pile of dance silks somewhere within your reach. You can dim the lights and ask the dancers to close their eyes. *Invite the Holy Spirit to move in the class.*

First Phase – duration approximately five minutes

> Start dancing around the room in the open spaces between the dancers. You can use a piece of silk or any dance fabric as you dance. For safety reasons, I recommend avoiding the use of flags that have sticks.

Second Phase – duration approximately 1-2 minutes of ministry time per dancer

Kneel next to the dancers as God highlights them to you, or as you feel drawn to them. Lay your hands on their feet or on their forehead. Ask the Holy Spirit if He has a word He wants to give to the dancers. You can say a short prayer or an encouraging word out loud to them. Or you can just lay your hands on them in stillness. In order to remember who you have already blessed, you can cover the dancers you've already ministered to with a silk or a piece of fabric. Then pick a new silk, and go to the next dancer God is highlighting for you. Repeat this until you have blessed all the dancers. If you have a bigger group of dancers to bless, it's helpful if you have interns or other helpers who can join you in blessing people. In this case, it's helpful if the people who are assisting you also leave a silk over the dancers they have blessed, so everyone knows who has already received ministry and who still needs it.

My comments on this exercise:

This is more of a prayer time than an exercise. I wanted to conclude this manual with an example of ministry time with a group of dancers. It's very important for the dancers to learn how to rest and relax in God's presence and just receive. You can encourage the dancers to turn their affections to God and receive directly from the Holy Spirit while they are lying down. This helps them to focus on His presence, rather than just wait for someone to minister to them.

A prayer of impartation

Father, in the Name of Jesus, I release an impartation of the grace and the anointing You have given me and blessed me with as a dance pastor. Thank You that freely I have received and freely I can give. I release the anointing to operate from a place of a heart to heart connection with You, to pastor and lead others into deeper intimacy with Jesus, being constantly led by the Holy Spirit. May Your Kingdom come with power as we minister with love, and may Your Son Jesus receive a Bride who is set free to worship with everything She is, without fear or shame!

About Saara Taina

Saara Taina was born in Finland and has been teaching worship dance for more than 15 years on five continents. She was a student in the School of Worship in Jerusalem, Israel, and studied dance in Sydney, Australia. She has an Advanced Diploma of Creative Arts in Christian Ministry, specializing in Contemporary Dance. Saara is an ordained minister of the Gospel by the River International Revival Network and she is currently pastoring the dance ministry teams at Bethel Healing Rooms and Bethel School of Supernatural Ministry in Redding, California. Saara travels extensively and her passion is to equip the global Bride of Christ to worship Jesus with everything She is, without fear or shame and to release the Kingdom of Heaven through dance and creativity. Saara is the author of *Encountering God Through Dance*.

Notes: